New Sun Rising

New Sun Rising: Stories for Japan

An anthology of stories, poems, photography and artwork
to celebrate the people of Japan

First published in 2012

by

RAGING AARDVARK PUBLISHING, Brisbane, Australia
© Raging Aardvark Publishing, 2012

ALL RIGHTS RESERVED
http://ragingaardvark.com

ISBN 978-0-9871383-1-6

Cover Images: © Daniel Werneck
Cover Design by Daniel Werneck
Section headings brush paintings ©Annie Evett

http://storiesforjapan.blogspot.com

Contents

Myths, Fables and Legends

Old and New

City Stories

Visitors

Outside Japan

Artwork

Contributors

Acknowledgements

Foreword

"On March 11, 2011 a devastating earthquake and tsunami struck the north of Japan. In the wake of one of the most catastrophic natural disasters in the history of Japan, a state of nuclear emergency was declared, forcing the evacuation of thousands more. The world watched, stunned. We wanted to help. Just giving money didn't seem like enough. The idea for New Sun Rising: Stories for Japan, a collection of stories and poems and art honouring and celebrating Japan, was born."

With these words, Frankie Sachs started the project. From a flurry of tweets and emails, New Sun Rising: Stories for Japan was off and running. The response was enormous and Frankie was inundated with offers of assistance. She quickly formed a tight group of editors and project assistants to work through the submissions and begin laying out the anthology.

Then life got crazy for everyone, the project stumbled and around October 2011, contact was lost with Frankie and some of her team. But Frankie's idea, the generosity of hundreds who sent in work and of the just over 60 contributors retained, together with all the hard work already done on the project and the support received, showed us that we had to go on. The world wasn't watching so much anymore. But people in Japan were still suffering from the effects of the disaster.

In February 2012 a small group got together to continue the anthology. And then came the first anniversary of the disaster. Although still difficult to calculate, it has been claimed that an estimated 19,000 people were killed. Dozens of communities were obliterated. Sources believe that more than 3,000 still remain missing. And what about the forgotten people? There were reports of a former nun taking in the homeless and neglected, of elderly people going to Fukushima to offer support. Uplifting stories.

The work in New Sun Rising: Stories for Japan is also predominantly uplifting. It is our way of celebrating Japan and its people through images and words.

We are honoured to have award-winning Austrian poet, Friederike Mayröcker, donate a poem in original German with English translation to this anthology. A major collection of her poems, Raving Language: Selected Poems 1946-2006 (trans. Richard Dove), was published by Carcanet Press, Manchester, UK in 2007. Mayröcker's poem can be seen as a bridge between why this anthology was created and the work donated by more than 60 contributors, several of whom have also contributed work to the New Sun Rising blog.

At the end of this book you will find a list of contributors and their bios. You will also find our acknowledgements to all those who helped this project on its way into the world.

It was a very difficult decision as to the charity or organisation to which we'd like to donate. It was agreed right from the beginning to contribute to an internationally recognised and reputable organisation which had the ability to assist a wide range of people. 100% of the proceeds raised from selling this anthology will be directed to the Japanese Red Cross Society.

We hope that you enjoy this book and that you will help us reach out to as many people as you can. Every reader counts. And we know that the blessings from those in need in a country that perhaps is, or could have been yours and ours, will far outnumber the help we all have to offer.

Sincerely, and on behalf of the whole team,

The Editors

Cherry Blossom by Catherine Edmunds
(pencil drawing)

Friederike Mayröcker

nämlich die Murmeltiere der feenhafte Mai ich meine dieser feenhafte Frühling im Blauglockenbaum ("auf einer kroatischen Wiese . . ")
es hat mir früher immer das Herz herausgerissen aber jetzt ist
alles egal, weiszt du alles egal, die "horen" von Schiller weiszt du
"ich lechze ja nach jeder Zeile von Ihnen." während die japanischen
Katzen nämlich die Katzen weinen eigentlich wehen : wehklagen weiszt
du alles egal, Schillers "horen", habe den Knall liege auf meinen
Armen in der Sonne im Fenster, rieche den Regen welcher eingesickert
viele Jahre in den Rahmen des Fensters, dünn wie von Schleiern mein
Schlaf, gegen Morgen zerreiszend, der Wind nämlich dieses Lüftchen
bläst in meinen Nacken (in der Ligusterhecke) so feenhafter Mai usw.
frisch wie damals in D. das Wehen des Mai da wir aus dem Haus
traten und Hand in Hand und die Perlen der Morgenröte habe den Knall
liege auf meinen Armen im Fenster rieche den Duft der vielen Regen
welche gesickert in den Holzrahmen des Fensters . . . . was
die Augenschlitze der Katzen angeht welche in der Zone = Sperrzone
umherirren und weinen und schreien ich meine der blaue Mai : Übung
des Mai »étude« ach Übung der Vögelchen »étude« bei Sonnenunter-
gang usw., es sichelt die Nacht, Kralle des Notenheftes, Kniestrümpfe
der Bäume auf einem Friedhof also von Efeu, so verlottertes Leben, le
kitsch, kl.gefaltetes Briefchen auf dem WC . . . . . . "so fuhr das in
mich obn auf einer höhe . . . . . " Thomas Kling

12.5.2011

(Translation: Liselotte Pope-Hoffmann)

namely the marmots the fairylike May I mean this fairylike spring in the blue foxglove tree ("on a Croatian meadow. . ")
it always used to tear out my heart but now nothing matters
any more, you know nothing matters, the "horen" by Schiller you know
"I do yearn for each line of yours". while the Japanese
cats namely the cats are weeping actually waving : wailing you
know nothing matters, Schiller's "horen", am off the rocker am lying on
my arms in the sun in the window, smelling the rain which has soaked
many years into the frame of the window, thin as of veils my
sleep, tearing towards morning, the wind namely this little breeze
is blowing into my neck (in the privet hedge) such fairylike May etc.
fresh like back then in D. the waving of May when out of the house
we stepped hand in hand and the pearls of dawn am off the rocker
am lying on my arms in the window smelling the scent of the many rains
which have soaked into the wooden frame of the window............. as
for the eye-slits of the cats which in the ZONE = forbidden zone
are wandering about and weeping and crying I mean the blue May : exercise
of May <étude> oh exercise of the little birds <étude> at sunset etc., the night is sickleing, claw of the music book, knee socks
of trees on a cemetery of ivy that is, such dissipated life, le
kitsch, little folded letter in the lavatory. . . . . . . "thus it struck
me up 'pon a height. . . . ." Thomas Kling

12.5.2011

Family Business

The Brewer's Son
a story by Lily Mulholland

Hisoka stamped his feet to shed the snow that caked his boots. He opened the heavy wooden door and entered the vestibule. Drawing woolen mitts from his hands, he muttered expletives as frigid fingers failed to grasp the strings that bound the leather to his feet. He managed to obtain purchase on one stubborn tail and pulled, then another from the other foot. Boots off, he slid open the inner door and dived into the warmth his mother managed to stoke in the house through even the whitest of winters.

The sound of her voice did not startle him; she would have been expecting him home this past hour. As a quiet, punctual boy, he had not given his parents any trouble. Now a man, the only son of the district's head sake brewer, Hisoka could detect the concern in the voice that called to him from the kitchen. His father would by now be seated in the central room of the house, adorned in the robe his mother kept warmed in the darkening afternoons in anticipation of her husband's arrival. As Hokkaido prefecture *tōji*, the patriarch's position in society was secure; Hisoka's mother knew her place.

"Hisoka-*kun*? Is that you home?"

"Yes, *Okāsan*." He scuttled into the room that housed his bed, pulling off his outer clothes and sliding on the slippers at the end of the futon. Hisoka knew what was coming next and was ready.

"Your father wishes to see you."

"Yes, *Okāsan.*"

Hisoka made the sign of obeisance as he entered the living space. Seated before him was the rotund body of his father, the stiff cotton kimono that swaddled his girth accentuating the man's unusual size. He did not look up as his son entered the room, preferring instead to attend to the papers piled on the table. Hisoka recognised his father's tactics and took the moment to admonish the rising fear and to urge himself to courage.

"A good day today, Hisoka," the man said as he tidied the sheaf of papers, banging their bottom edges against the table. A general calling his troops to order.

"Yes, *Otōsan.*"

"All is ready for my inspection tomorrow?"

"Yes, *Otōsan.*"

"You have seen to everything yourself?"

"Three hundred and six crates, *Otōsan.* Everything exactly as ordered by the royal palace."

Hisoka could feel a filial fire burning in his face. He had worked hard, determined to prove to his father he too would be a worthy *tōji* when the time came. He dared to look at his father, hoping to see a hint of warmth infuse the furrowed face before launching into the question he had prepared so carefully.

"Father!"

"You cannot marry her." It was an executioner's blow.

Unable to hide hurt and confusion, Hisoka snapped his chin to his chest and bowed. It was the sign of respect he had made to his father since he could walk; a reflex action against which Hisoka's will was no match.

"*Hai.*"

Hisoka bowed again and escaped the room, bursting past his younger sister who had no time to blush at being caught eavesdropping through the paper walls. She made to follow him as he headed out through the foyer.

"Not now, Etsuko-*kun*." He kicked off the slippers and grabbed his coat and boots.

"But Hisoka, where are you going?"

"Not now, little one." He paused on the veranda and pulled on the boots, leaving the laces loose. Jamming arms into coat sleeves, he trudged out into the snow-laden night. He did not look back, choosing instead to increase the length of his stride, the desire to put distance between him and his father propelling him further into the darkness.

"Where is Hisoka?" demanded Masato as the evening meal was placed before him. The adjacent place was empty. The man picked up a pair of lacquered chopsticks and jabbed their tips into the food, testing the rice for stickiness and the *nori* for strength.

"He has gone out", said his wife quietly as she prepared to withdraw from the room.

He waggled his chopsticks at her. "What do you mean 'gone out'?"

Junko found herself on a precipice: for twenty-eight years she had remained silent, acceding to her husband's many demands. She jumped.

"Masato-*san*," she said in a firm voice she did not recognise as her own, "your son is a man."

"You speak to me, woman?" He stared at her, laden chopsticks half-way between bowl and mouth.

Junko could not fathom the look on her husband's face; a mirthless man is hard to read. Not for the first time she mourned the man she had married. She took a deep breath.

"I speak to you as the mother of your only son. I speak to you as your life's companion. I speak to you as the girl you fell in love with when we were young."

Masato closed his eyes. He was back in the sake factory of his youth, his father a tiger prowling the floors, waiting to pounce should the time-honoured brewing process be breached. The *tōji* recalled the wall of his father's heart and how he had worked his fingers raw, proving his value to the family business. He remembered Junko, the girl who had stolen his heart as she flicked tiny balls of sake mash into his hair when he wasn't looking. He remembered his father's stony refusal when he sought the matrimonial blessing. And Masato remembered the solemn promise he made those many years ago: I will cherish my son and he will know his father's love. His eyes popped open.

"Bring me Etsuko."

Junko's brows dipped.

"Don't look so worried, wife. I only want her to tell me where he is. That damned girl knows everything."

Junko couldn't be certain, but she thought she saw the shadow of a smile cross her husband's face.

Himitsu Bako
a poem by W.F. Lantry

We hold the mystery within our hands.
We cannot fabricate the thing itself,
but we can build a box to hold it still.
The decoration's marquetry, the trick
is hiding mechanisms in the grain.
Push here, slide this, the top becomes the base.

And quickly, we forget what's held inside.
Or can't remember why we ever sought
to open this thing made with skillful hands.
We lose ourselves within the patterned grain
turning the ornament that mystifies
the joinery we thought to clarify.

It does no good to watch what others do,
note where they press or pull, see how the hinge
becomes a wedge to push the tiny beam
along its path, marked by contrasting wood.
We must divine the stratagem ourselves
and understand the nature of the mind

who made this inlaid artifice, and carved
each piece to fit correctly through its maze
in asymmetric sequence, intricate
and fabricated to be beautiful
in its own workings, only giving up
what it contains to patient careful hands.

The Ambassador of Foreign Affairs
a story by Marylee MacDonald

Sun filtered through the redwoods and fell on the hotel balcony where Kiyoshi Tanaka held a black mug in his palsied hands. Stretching his legs to rid them of cramps, he blew on his tea, sipped, and hoped the caffeine would carry him through dinner. Only three hours before, his plane had landed in San Francisco; he'd made it safely to the eastern shore of the Pacific, his first time in America, and tonight, he would meet the family of the groom. His daughter Mayumi, thirty-seven, shivered and buttoned her sweater.

"Up here in Marin County," she said, "it's always foggy."

"Is it warmer where you live?" he asked.

"Much," she said, "but in Sunnyvale, the sky's so brown, you can hardly see across the bay."

Despite the fog, it was beautiful here in Mill Valley. Mist rose from the stream below them. Shrouds wrapped the trees.

"Do you know what they are?" Mayumi said, nodding toward the forest.

"Sempervirens," he said. Always living, but fossils, like himself. Japonica or sequoia? He put his cup on the table. After huffing on his lenses and wiping them with his handkerchief, he stood and peered into the dusk. Sequoia, no doubt. The trees grew admirably straight and joined at the sky. Birds twittered. He felt a haiku coming and patted his pocket. Regrettably, his notebook was in the room.

"I remember..." Mayumi whispered.

He knew what she was thinking: her mother's love of redwoods, the sacred *sugi* that sacrificed themselves to provide the beams of ancient temples. An old poem came to mind.

I see her only from afar

For she is lofty

Like the divine *sugi*

By the shrine at Miwa.

Many are the nights I sleep alone.

Resting against the balcony, he folded his arms. Caring for Chiyo had worn him out. Seven months had gone by since her death, and his enthusiasm for life had not returned. At Mayumi's urging, he had decided to extend his stay, but he could not stay forever.

Mayumi looked up at him. "You're not drinking your tea."

His tea was cool by now. "It tastes..."

"Stale?"

"A little." He leaned over for his cup.

"You don't have to drink it." She snatched the mug away and threw the contents over the rail.

This was an unfamiliar tone.

"The tea was only slightly bitter," he said.

"No, no, no. Very bitter." Mayumi dumped out her own cup, doubled over, and began rocking. Through hair hanging around her face, he saw her wipe her eyes. "I do not have to drink the bitter cup!" she said. "No one can make me."

"No one is forcing you to marry."

"Immigration is."

Not another disrupted engagement! One had been enough. He handed her a folded handkerchief. "Here once again at the *basho* tree, my sleeves are soaked with tears."

She sniffed a laugh. "So do you think the frog should leap in the pond again?" she said.

"That depends."

"Father, ever the diplomat."

"He is a *gaijin*," he said, "but not all of them are boorish."

"If I want to marry, this is my last chance."

"*So desu*," he said.

Like hulls of rice in a burlap sack, weariness shifted through Tanaka's body. During his wife's long illness, he had begun seeking truths in the poems he had memorized as a young man. Basho wrote that it was rare for anyone to reach the age of seventy. The period when mind and body truly flourished was not much more than twenty years. In anticipation of his flight to California, Tanaka had reread the poet's great works, Account of a Weather-Beaten Skeleton and The Narrow Road to Oku, preparing himself for this separation from the one person who meant most to him. His wife was gone. Mayumi was all he had left.

"What should I do?" she said.

"You came here to live with him."

"Live, yes."

"But not marry."

"He is weak."

"*So desu*," he said.

"I need someone solid." She looked up, eyes glittering. "A rock."

He waited. Maybe she had decided to come back to Japan. But what would be her future: her old job at Berlitz, dinner with her father, watching her girlfriends raise their children? His life was nearing its end, but there was much she had left to experience.

Sighing, Mayumi stood. "We should go. Ian's mother bought tickets to this dinner-dance. 'Real America,' she calls it."

Tanaka picked up the chairs. "First, the rock must wash his hands."

The American Legion Log Cabin Post 179 was a large, two-story building made from pine trees notched at the ends. Smoke, infused with the smell of fatty pork, turned the sky an eerie white.

Hesitating to cross the parking lot, Tanaka asked, "Is the building on fire?"

13

Mayumi laughed. "No. It's a barbecue."

Barbecue. His nose tingled.

Mayumi flipped open her cell phone. "Ian, where in hell are you?"

Mayumi was angry. That was a bad sign. If she did not treat her fiancé well, he might walk away. Her first fiancé, brother of Mayumi's best friend, had not been patient with the outbursts, and shortly after Tanaka had put down a deposit on the wedding-hotel, the groom's mother had called to 'discuss the future'. She had been witness to one too many of Mayumi's tantrums.

Mayumi had stayed in her room for months, claiming she would never fall in love again. Young people! This word 'love'--what did it mean? His circumstances had been different, a matter of survival after the war. For his wife Chiyo, a widow four years his senior, marriage had been a chance to start over. Many decisions in life came from opportunities that landed in your lap and not from choice at all.

As they approached the building, he looked through the downstairs windows into a noisy, crowded tavern.

"Don't worry," Mayumi said. "We're going upstairs."

"Fine," he said, looking up at a balcony. He heard music.

The stairs were steep and rose to the unknown. He paused to catch his breath.

"Are you okay?" Mayumi said.

"*Daijyobu*," he said, though in truth, the smoke hurt his lungs.

Mayumi flipped open her cell phone. "Come help my dad."

He put up a hand. "*Iranai*." He did not want to show weakness before his son-in-law. There were only ten more steps.

Shortly before her mother's death, Mayumi had brought Ian to the apartment. He was one of her 'tutees', Mayumi said, and she wanted him to practice his Japanese. For the occasion, Tanaka had dressed Chiyo in a silk bathrobe and brought her to the living room, putting two cushions on the floor to keep her bones from coming through her flesh. Ian arrived, a slight young man: round-eyed, pink cheeked. Polite, Tanaka thought, but unremarkable.

When they departed, Chiyo said, "He is more than her student."

Tanaka said he was too young. "They will learn to care for each other," Chiyo said, sighing with relief as he placed her down on the futon. "We did."

Upstairs, Tanaka stood at the door. Men shouted. Chairs screeched. It was like the Tokyo Fish Market. On the stage, three cowboys with guitars stood at microphones. There was a man playing a violin, though he played it badly, bowing across several strings at once. There were a hundred metal tables and folding chairs, and a U-shaped space near the stage for dancers. No one had started yet. People were eating.

Ian came toward them, his smile a reflex, like the kick after a doctor's knee-tap, and Tanaka remembered that Americans always smiled, even for no reason. Tanaka bowed. "You made it," Ian said, clasping Tanaka's hand in both of his. "Great to see you again."

Tanaka had forgotten Ian's curly hair. The boy looked like a politician. So undignified: men with permanents.

"Come on," Ian said, turning back the way he'd come. "My mom is dying to meet you."

"*Ashi de matoi*," Mayumi muttered.

A drag? Ian's mother? This was disrespectful.

Ian took her hand and smiled. "I missed you," he said.

Mayumi turned her cheek, and he kissed it.

They were headed for a table near the stage, where Tanaka saw an attractive woman with hair like yellow cotton-candy. She was seated and staring at him.

"That's my mom," Ian said. "She's had ants in her pants all day."

Tanaka thought of his *haiku* teacher, Yoko Sugawa, who taught that an ant was like Basho's frog. Ten poets looking at the same ant would write ten different poems. In seventeen syllables, he had described his ant, an exoskeleton in three parts--the head, thorax, and abdomen. When he had read his poem, Mrs. Sugawa sat in silence. Then, finally, she said, "Let us look not at our ants but rather into them. If we pay attention, surely the ant will speak to us." So far, his ant had remained silent.

The woman scooted back from the table and stood, hands on hips. Her smile snapped into place. Even a small ant, like the sugar ants that found their way to his fourth floor walk-up, could not have managed to crawl up the leg of her jeans. She wore a white, long-sleeved shirt. Two pointy cones that looked like drinking water cups stood out from her chest. Ian introduced them. His mother's name was Carol.

Tanaka bowed.

"Get outta here!" Ian's mother grabbed his hand. "Mayumi, you didn't tell us your father was so *galant*." There were four places at the table. She pulled her chair around to his side and, once seated, he felt her thigh press against his leg.

"By the end of the weekend," she said, "we're going to be bosom buddies."

Bosom, he thought, nearly breathless, but managed to gasp out the phrase he had rehearsed. "This is a momentous occasion for both our families."

"Darn right!" she said. "I'm so tickled Ian met a sweet little girl like Mayumi."

"She is woman," Tanaka said, a woman well beyond marriageable age, he could have added, but didn't. At home, thirty-seven was 'old Christmas cake'.

"Well, she looks like a girl to me," Carol said. "How old are you, Honey? Ian's such a gentleman. He won't say."

"That is private information," Mayumi said. "I wish you would not keep asking."

Carol held up her hands. "Hey, hey! No offense."

Ian's lips stretched sideways like large rubber bands, and when he looked down, his chin disappeared inside the collar of his shirt.

Poor boy. Tanaka wondered if he should do something.

Ian ran his fingers through his hair. "I didn't realize you spoke English, Sir."

"Oh, yes," Carol said. "Your English is perfect."

"My written English is better than my spoken," he said.

"He worked in the Ministry of Foreign Affairs," Mayumi said.

"That sounds like our State Department!" Carol clapped her hands. "We'll have to call you Mr. Ambassador, the Ambassador of Foreign Affairs."

"But I was only a..."

Don't swallow the worm, Mayumi said in Japanese. He looked at her, frowned, and cocked his head. She looked back, thin-lipped. He was only going to explain that he was a low-level bureaucrat, stuck translating agricultural treaties.

"Did you bring a tuxedo?" Carol said.

Tanaka nodded.

"Good," Carol said, "because you're mine now, and I get to show you off."

"How do you mean?" Tanaka said.

"You're a status symbol," Mayumi said. "A trophy."

"My father is rich," Ian said.

"That's putting it mildly," Carol said. "He's filthy rich. And, he ran off with my best friend. They bought this place up at Sea Ranch and left me with a crappy, three-bedroom condo in Mill Valley."

He thought about the word 'Valley'. It was hard to pronounce. Double 'els' had always given him problems. He wanted to thank her for placing him near the Sempervirens sequoia. The mist, the creek, everything was wonderful, and tomorrow, he would wake up and look at it with the benefit of dawn.

"I am enjoying Mill...the hotel you arranged," he said. "The bed seems very comfortable."

"Well, good," Carol said. "Make me an offer I can't refuse."

An offer? What sort of offer? Tanaka looked at Mayumi. She shrugged and rolled her eyes.

Two men in black leather jackets took a table by the dance floor. One had a long, white braid and a mustache like a Chinese Emperor. He glanced over.

Carol jerked a thumb at them. "That's my old beau," she said. "I seem to have a way of picking them." The old boyfriend folded his arms and turned his back.

"Let's annoy him." Carol put two fingers in her mouth and whistled.

A heavy woman in a stained apron came to the table, looking at them with a smirk. "Had a few, Carol?"

"We'll take the barnyard platter." Carol held up four fingers. "And bring some brewskies."

"I didn't even have a chance to look at the menu," Mayumi said.

"The barnyard's what everyone's having," Carol said. "This here's a fundraiser they do once a year. The Vets set up smokers out back, and it's the best damn barbecue you'll ever eat."

"Vets?" Tanaka said, looking from Ian to Carol.

"War Veterans," Carol said. "But don't worry. You're safe--unless you're a kamikaze pilot. You're not, are you?"

"I was fourteen when the war ended," Tanaka said. "My first job was working for the Army of Occupation."

"What is this 'barnyard platter'?" Mayumi said.

"You're not a vegetarian, are you?" Carol said. "If so, there's corn on the cob."

"I hope it's not spicy." Mayumi looked at Ian.

"Not too," he said. "Oh, and Mr. Tanaka, with barbecue, it's polite to eat with your fingers."

"Thank you for explaining," Tanaka said. He had never heard of anyone, with the possible exception of Koreans and Africans, eating meat with their fingers.

Ian leaned over. "Did Mayumi tell you about my mom?"

"Tell him what about your mom?" Carol said.

"That you're a party animal," Ian said, looking at her.

Party animal. Tanaka frowned. Was this related to 'barnyard'?

"What you see is what you get," Ian said.

"She is out of control," Mayumi muttered under her breath in Japanese.

"I believe the expression is 'free spirit,'" Tanaka said. "Is that correct?"

Carol, looking pleased, shrugged as if trying on new clothing. "I'll take that as a compliment."

Ian laughed. "Truly, you are a diplomat."

Carol gestured toward the stage. "We're being watched."

A lone cowboy sat on a stool. He was chewing a toothpick.

Tanaka straightened himself and picked up his beer. A full liter. "What time must I be ready for the wedding?"

"Noon," Ian said.

"I am curious to see the ceremony."

"It'll be outdoors," Ian said. "All our friends are coming." He took Mayumi's hand and gazed at her with a look of longing. "I wish your mother could have lived to share our joy."

Speaking Japanese, Mayumi said, "He doesn't know this is inauspicious."

"Poor lady," Carol said. "Did she suffer at the end?"

Tanaka looked at the ceiling. There were several dark stains, as if a bottle had exploded, and smoke rings around the circular vents.

"I understand. It hurts right here." Carol thumped her chest. "You Japanese hold everything inside. Sometimes, it's better to let it all hang out." She shook her hands as if they were limp rags.

"Mom," Ian said, "I don't think this is something they want to discuss. Dinner's here."

Carol moved the saltshakers. A stack of paper plates, a pile of rolled-up napkins, and a metal platter landed on the tabletop. Tanaka stared at the wings and haunches, but watched what Ian's mother did, and when she reached with her fingers for a quarter chicken--no hot towels to clean hands, no trips to the wash room--he grabbed a steak as big as his shoe. At home, a steak this size would feed a sumo wrestler. However, he was in America. He bit off a corner, then saw Ian's mouth gape open.

Mayumi giggled behind her hand. "You should use a knife and fork."

He looked at the napkins. Plastic silverware was in them. The utensils were white, he wanted to explain. Heat rising on his neck, Tanaka put the steak down and wiped his fingers. His lips burned. The sauce must contain hot pepper. He gulped down beer, but that made the burning worse. He wiped his lips, cleared his throat, and pulled at the knot of his necktie. There was no food in Japan, not even pure wasabi squeezed from a tube, that could burn a hole in your tongue this fast.

The man Carol said was watching them approached the table. He removed his hat. "I just came over to say '*Kon'nichi wa*' and '*Sayonara*.'"

Tanaka stood and bowed. "Good evening." He wondered why the man was wishing him 'good afternoon' and 'goodbye'. Strange *gaijin*, Tanaka thought, sitting down. What an experience this was!

Carol finished her beer, looked at the stage, and, catching the eye of the lead singer, jerked her thumb toward the dance floor, and shouted. "Let's get the party started."

"I don't feel like dancing," Ian said.

"If you dance," Carol said, "I'll limit myself to one glass of champagne at the wedding."

"Okay, one dance, Mom," Ian said. "Then we're going. You've had too much to drink."

"One beer?" she said.

"And three bourbon sours while we were waiting."

"Come on, Mayumi," Carol said. "Don't be a stick in the mud. Dance with the Ambassador."

Tanaka had seen his daughter throw a plate across the room. She looked as if she were about to do that now. "It's only a cheap one," she had reassured her mother, who had risen up on an elbow to see what shattered. Mayumi, as reliable as a hand-wound clock, was also sprung-tight. An invitation to a baby shower had triggered her outburst. One by one, her friends had married, and when babies arrived, they could no longer go out with her. Before she'd met Ian, Mayumi had spent most evenings at home. Tanaka stood and offered his hand.

Mayumi started to refuse, then looked at Ian.

He had a pleading look in his eyes.

"Oh, all right," she said, and then in Japanese, "I'm just humoring him."

"Small gesture, large kindness," Tanaka said.

Other women scooted their chairs out, wiped their hands, and pushed the piles of bones away. A song began. It was one he recognized, *The Tennessee Waltz*. Tanaka had learned ballroom dance as part of his Ministry training and enjoyed the waltz. Mayumi had never learned, and she moved like a *Bunraki* puppet, hands limp, arms like wooden sticks. The only time he'd ever seen her dance was in her bedroom; her mother had been in the hospital to have a lump removed. Mayumi had turned up the phonograph's volume and pumped her arms until her eyes rolled and she fell on the floor, exhausted. It looked like a seizure, but when Tanaka knelt and brushed back her bangs, she smiled. "That felt good."

He did not understand why she'd had these periodic explosions. Her mother never had them. America might be a better fit. When the music stopped, Tanaka bowed and walked his daughter to the table. He tucked a napkin in his shirt and fell to the task of scraping sauce off the steak. His top denture had come loose. The adhesive was back in his suitcase, and he pressed his thumb against his plate, trying to get it to reattach.

Ian, holding a chicken drumstick and pointing at the food, asked a bus boy to "box up a doggie bag." Tanaka knew about this tradition. In the years he worked at the Ministry's Tokyo office, he had often played host to delegations of chicken farmers, and they never left food on their plates. The bus boy returned with the leftovers.

The lights dimmed. A mirrored globe began to revolve and throw sparkles. "Let's pick up the pace," the lead singer said. "This next one's for all you Two-Steppers." The band began to play. The tempo was fast. Ian's mother went over to the man on the stool, and after a brief conversation, he joined her on the dance floor. Catching her hand, he dipped and swung her around. As Tanaka watched her footwork, he decided that the dance steps were not a fox trot, but closer to a cha-cha-cha. Every few steps, she took a little hop, came down, and swung around, guided by her partner, who flung her away from him, then yanked her back, so that she curled into his arm. He was not exerting himself, and his posture was not the normal dance position--erect. When he expected to receive her, he curved his back slightly at the shoulders, and when he flung her away, he straightened up, the heel of his cowboy boot coming down on the floor, as if to say, "There! Take that!"

Under the table, Tanaka's feet began to move. Carol was an excellent dancer; she knew how to follow a man's lead. The band changed tempo. A waltz again. He stood, determined to cut in.

Ian intercepted him. "I'm sorry, Mr. Tanaka. This is dragging on. We'll get you home."

"It is a good party," he said.

"I'm tired," Mayumi said. "Ian, call your mother."

Tanaka frowned. That tone in his daughter's voice was getting under his skin. He wanted to dance.

Outside in the parking lot, the full moon cast shadows.

"Are you all right to drive?" Ian asked his mother.

"Fine," she said. "You take Mayumi and the Ambassador back to the hotel."

Tanaka wished Carol a good night's sleep and bowed "good night" to her dance partner. The two headed toward a black, Ford F250 truck. Ian ran across the gravel and demanded to know where she was going. Tanaka stood by his daughter's Camry. The mother, he gathered, was arguing that they might go to another place and dance.

"Drive your own car, then," Ian said.

"I'll come back for it," Carol said.

Mayumi called across the parking lot. "Ian, my father is tired."

That was true. Tanaka got in the back seat, the leather sighing beneath him. Reaching in his pocket for his pill-box, his hands shook. He pried the top off and put the pills in his mouth, one at a time, then spread his fingers and hoped to see the shaking stop. Across the top of his skull, he felt a prickling sensation. Even though he was tired, the evening had been remarkable. Until just this instant, he hadn't thought about his frailty or whether there was any point to life, a reason to go on. Quite remarkable.

"Ian!" Mayumi shouted. "I'm leaving." She stood by the passenger door, then slammed it, and stomped toward the driver's side.

Ian ran to the car, jumped in, and revved the engine.

"Get in!" Ian's voice changed octaves like a boy who has not fully grown into manhood.

Mayumi slid into the front seat and closed the door.

Roaring out of the parking lot, Ian followed the truck. "Write down that license number!"

"The hotel's the other way," Mayumi said.

"I have to follow them," Ian said.

"Turn around. Now, Ian, before I get angry."

"Just write down that license."

"The truck is making too much dust," Mayumi said.

The dust was like a snowstorm. Tanaka felt a bump and heard the hum of tires. When the Toyota emerged from the cloud, he saw they were on a winding road, going through the mountains.

"Did you get it?" Ian screamed.

"Get what," Mayumi said. "I couldn't see anything."

"I think they went the other way," Tanaka said.

Ian turned into a driveway. "I'll drop you off and go find her." Then, looking in the rear view mirror, he said, "Do you need anything, Tanaka-san?"

Tanaka could not avoid the frightened eyes that sought his understanding. His stomach growled.

"*Udon*," he said.

"Why don't you give it up?" Mayumi said.

"That guy could be a serial killer," Ian said.

"The guy's in more danger than your mother," Mayumi said. "She's just making a fool of herself."

No, Tanaka thought. She was bringing shame on the family. Only a man could understand the power a woman had to rob him of dignity.

At the hotel, Tanaka saw that someone had been in his room. The lights were dim, and on the white quilt sat a small square of dark chocolate. Grateful, he unwrapped the foil and felt the chocolate melt on his tongue. The sweetness lasted through his shower. He toweled dry, put on pajamas, and after filling a water glass, removed his teeth. He was about to turn out the light when he heard a drawer slam. It was from Mayumi's room. A second slam shook his mirror.

He sat on the bed, his feet dangling above the rug. He listened. Silence. He slid off the bed and into his slippers, padding around. He rubbed his chin. There was mole. From it, long hairs grew. He had depended on his wife to snip the strands with her manicure scissors. He had hoped his daughter might be willing to do it.

He put on a robe and, then remembered his dentures. Outside Mayumi's door, he gave three, brisk raps.

She looked out. "Oh, it's you."

"May I come in?"

She stood aside. "I'll make tea."

"Black will keep me awake."

"I have o-cha."

At a double sink by the closet, there was a coffee maker; she poured in water, and he heard the water hiss and drip. Suitcases stood beside the dresser. Ian's clothes were heaped on the bed. Sitting on one of two chairs by the door, Tanaka rested his elbow on the table.

"When do you expect him back?" Tanaka said.

"Soon," she said.

"What will you do then?"

"Leave." Mayumi carried over two cups and sat down.

"Where will you go?"

"The hotel's not full. I have money."

"Tomorrow is your wedding."

"He can have it without me."

Tanaka brought the cup to his lips. In the steam, he could smell a hint of grass. This was the way Chiyo would have prepared it. Nodding to his tea, he said, "A man and a woman need each other in many small ways."

"I cannot marry," she said. "I'm too upset."

Tanaka looked into his tea cup. Sediment had escaped the bag and collected in the bottom.

"If you do not marry him, you will bring dishonor on your family."

"What family?" she snorted.

"Me," he said.

"I thought you would be happy."

"I will be, if you are content."

"I want to come home. I miss my country."

"When you came here, did you love him?"

"After mother's death, I would have done anything to leave that apartment."

"Why?" he said.

"It was dark and sad."

"Did you love him when you accepted his proposal?"

"I guess you could say, I hoped I could."

"I wondered about the age difference."

"He doesn't know my age."

"How old does he think you are?"

"Twenty-nine."

"How fast the clock turns back."

Mayumi shrugged. "I don't think he would care."

"Then what is the problem?"

"His mother."

"She is busy with own life," Tanaka said. "She will not interfere." He put his cup down, then turned, drew back the curtain, and saw the Camry pull into an empty space. He watched Ian open the trunk and take something out.

"He can't stand up to her," Mayumi said.

Tanaka dropped the curtain. "This is women's business," he said. Women's business was generally ill conceived and petty, and he had no patience for the minor hurts and intrigues of women who did not like their husband's mothers.

A key turned in the lock.

"Ian!" Mayumi stood and threw her arms around him.

So much for not loving him. Mayumi looked happy, Ian pleased. What was love but a smile at the end of the day? It was simple.

"Hi, you two," Ian said, placing three white bags on the table. He unpacked wax containers of soup and handed out chopsticks. "I drove down the hill to a Japanese place. They were closing, but I pounded on the door and convinced them to give me some *udon*."

"Did you find her?" Mayumi said.

"She wasn't in the usual places," Ian said.

"The slut," Mayumi said in Japanese.

This had to stop, Tanaka thought. Her displays of temper were a disgrace. He was fed up. "*Sonna koto iwanai de kure. Kotchi made ki ga makeru ja nai ka.*"

Mayumi blinked as if she'd been slapped. Tears welled in her eyes. She looked at him.

He looked from her to the bed. Move, he thought, and to make sure she understood that she was not to use that tone of voice again, added, "*So darou.*"

"So it is," Ian nodded, "but the other thing you said, I didn't get."

"He was reminding me to have better manners," Mayumi said. "Please. Take this seat. You have had a stressful day."

She looked at Tanaka. He nodded.

"Thanks, Honey," Ian said. "You didn't tell me your father was such a kind man."

Tanaka watched his future son-in-law. Ian dipped chopsticks into his *udon*. He should lower his voice, not let it change register; he could turn his head and hide his feelings of upset, even if he could not make them disappear. Mayumi must show respect for her husband. Ian bit the noodle in half.

"Do it like this," Tanaka said in a gravelly voice, pulling the worm of a noodle through his lips. "*Tsu-rup, tsu-rup.* That is the verb for eating noodles." Trying to recall a Basho poem, he sucked another long one and moved his feet so that the three sets of knees touched. The poem came to him. For Ian's benefit, he translated.

"In this world of ours, we eat only to cast out, sleep only to wake, and what comes after is simply to die at last."

The noodles tasted good.

As Leaves Fall

haibun by Mark Kerstetter

One need only reach out and scoop up the names and colors at hand, shake them down into an eye- teasing, tantalizingly tenuous balance. Deny accident and roll with gravity. This method promises a prodigious output, a prolonged precocity of vision. Think Picasso, throwing gold coins to a crowd whose enthusiasm never diminishes. Think scratch-a-day, hiccup-a-day, think the camera going down into the very pores of a skin whose softness gave up its last secret.

building blocks of life

death's last seed falling

virgin hands

Japanese Block Print by Diane Stephenson
(block print, white/teal)

Cherry Blossoms Never Die
a story by Bard T. Fox Dunham

Grandfather stopped painting after Keiko's mother died. Everyday, walking home from school, she kept her eyes open for beautiful things for him to paint, hoping to inspire him to pick up his brush. She spotted a turtle by the side of the road. That would be a nice thing for Grandfather to paint. The lady at the store, where Keiko stopped to get tea, candy and tuna for Grandfather, had only three teeth and a lazy eye. Maybe Grandfather would like to paint her.

She hurried to get the tea and fish to her Grandfather before his visitor arrived. She climbed the hill to the cottage over Tosa Bay where Grandfather's family had lived for generations, living from the sea and the wares of their nets.

Grandfather's friend from America was coming today. Keiko had never met anyone from that far away, and she wondered if he would look like the Americans she had seen on television.

Grandfather had sent her to the shop to buy *Uji* tea. *Uji* being so expensive, he only served it when special guests came to visit, like when the director of the Museum of Art in Kochi came to their home to tell him he'd been named as a 'National Treasure' for his paintings. The director had asked Grandfather to paint something for the museum, but that was the year Grandmother and Mother died when their bodies got cancer. That's when Grandfather set down his brushes and left his painting of *sakura* trees in blossom inchoate in his studio.

"The fish were fresh?" Grandfather asked when Keiko got home.

"*Hai, ojii-san.*"

She laid the fish on the counter and handed Grandfather the box of tea. He took the tea in his slender hands—hands that guided a paintbrush the way wind guides a sail—and sniffed the tea. The tide had long since gone out in his eyes, but little things brought it back: the rich smell of green tea, Keiko's laughter, the moon preening on the ocean at night.

"I spotted a turtle on the road," she told him. "I'm sure he would like his portrait painted."

Grandfather took the broom to sweep the floor, but she could see him limping on his left leg. It rained in the morning, aggravating it. He'd been wounded in the war, but Keiko never knew how. Grandfather never spoke about the war, only that it's where he'd met the American. They shared many letters over the years.

Keiko offered her tiny hands to help with the sweeping, and he handed her the broom. She put on an apron to guard her navy-blue, school uniform from being soiled, then she went to work with the broom twice as tall as she.

"You are a good girl, Keiko. Your father will be home soon."

Keiko kept a photo of father and mother around her neck on a necklace she had woven of fronds and chrysanthemum stems. The picture had faded, washing away her mother's face, and Keiko could not remember it. She would sometimes imagine her with the face of a dolphin and dreamed at night her mother had come to take her to swim in the ocean.

"I have a surprise for you, Keiko. Your father is going to call you tonight."

She grinned, giving a little cheer and swept the room in half the time. Father worked on an oil platform off Karafuto island near Russia. As an important engineer, Keiko's father often worked out of the country, so she had come to live with her grandfather. She wouldn't like living out to sea because the ocean made her sick. One time, Grandfather took her fishing, and she emptied her stomach all over the boat. Grandfather said it must have been very lucky, because he caught four fish that morning.

"He will sing you *Edo Komoriuta* before you go to sleep like your mother did."

Keiko finished sweeping and started in the *ribingu*, the room where his guest would be entertained.

Grandfather filled a pot then set it to boil on the irori, placing it on a rack over the hot coals in the square pit. Grandmother always teased him about the sunken hearth, saying they should not be so backwards.

She hurried to finish sweeping before the American arrived.

"You met him in the war?"

"I met him in the ocean," Grandfather said.

"Were you both soldiers together?"

"Yes. We were brothers, and we were enemies."

Grandfather set out the *hohin* teapot, not the usual *kyusu* he used to brew tea. The *hohin* was smaller than the *kyushu* and had no handle. The white skin of the teapot looked cloud woven, azure water lilies floating in a pond painted on its side. The thinner spout allowed tiny tea leaves to be poured with the steeped water, enhancing the flavor. This was not a pot meant to make tea just for casual drinking; it was meant to nourish the soul. Grandfather's guest must be important.

"Go change out of your uniform," Grandfather said.

"*Hai, ojii-san.*"

Keiko had just finished dressing when she heard a tap at the door. She ran from her room, but remembered her poise, slowed her little legs and walked into the kitchen.

Grandfather slid open the door.

Tall as a cypress, the American ducked through the doorway. Keiko spied on him through the side of the hanging *noren*. He set down his satchel and took off his shoes in the *genkan* before coming into the house proper. His jowls sagged like melting snow banks, and his belly hung over his pants like a Buddha statue, getting in the way of his arms. He picked one of the pair of slippers left out for guests. Keiko wondered if all Americans had feet that big and clumsy. How could he walk on two tree stumps? He stretched the slippers over his feet, nearly toppling over when he lost his balance. Keiko stifled a giggle.

Grandfather bowed.

"Welcome Matthews-*san*."

"Mr. Moto-*san*," said Matthews-san.

"Please. I am Ichi to you."

He must have been a good friend indeed for Grandfather to honor him by allowing him to use his first name.

Because of Father's job as an engineer, he often worked with American and British companies, so he was fluent in English. He'd wanted Keiko to have an early advantage, so she'd grown up hearing two languages. This would help her when she started *juku* next year and give her a better score on the tests. She'd never spoken to an American before, only heard their music and seen their television shows. She was glad for the chance to practice the language.

"I'm mighty glad to be here," Matthews-*san* said.

She stifled another giggle, tickled by the American's accent. He reminded Keiko of a cowboy from some of the films she had seen. Did he live on a large ranch across the sea? With horses and cows?

From a satchel, Matthews-*san* removed three gifts, two wrapped in white paper.

"I've had a crash course on Japanese customs," he said to Grandfather. He handed Grandfather a box of dried fruits for the house and one of the wrapped gifts. Grandfather accepted the gift with both hands, then he bowed again and thanked him.

Keiko waited in the doorway, remaining silent as was her place, but questions filled her mouth like fish in a pond. She wanted to pull on his caterpillar lips and search the pockets of his gray raincoat to see the things he brought from America.

"I have another surprise coming, but it's late," Matthews-*san* said. "This is your granddaughter?"

"This is Keiko. Her father is away working on an oil platform."

Keiko, being invited into the conversation, went to Matthews-san. He knelt down and kissed her forehead. She blushed, not being used to such open affection from a stranger.

"Hello there, little lady. Your grandfather has written about you, told me you've got an ear for American music."

He handed Keiko the last gift. She held it in her hands, feeling the smooth surface beneath. It would be rude to open it unless insisted upon, so she had to wait.

"Go on then. Open her up."

Grandfather nodded. "You may do it American style."

She admired the wrapping paper and carefully pried it free without crinkling it. She looked through the CDs: Mariah Carey, Depeche Mode, U2."

"Thank you, Matthews-san," she said, bowing.

"She sure is pretty, Ichi," he said. "You must be proud."

"She is beautiful," said Grandfather. "But she doesn't always do her chores on time."

Matthews-san grinned.

"I have a grandson the same age," he said. "Perhaps you would like him."

"*Ojii-san* says you both met in the ocean."

Grandfather filled the *hohin* teapot with the steaming brew and set the pot and three thin bowls on the table. He beckoned for Matthews-san to sit down.

Grandfather poured the tea. The soothing aroma made Keiko sleepy.

"Sure did," Matthews-san replied. "Right smack in the middle of the deep blue sea. Your grandfather saved my life. Best man I know. Yes sir."

Lt. Commander Wilbur Matthews never saw the Zero that shot up his plane. It flew down out of the sun like a Phoenix, spraying him with machine gun fire, revenge for the devastation the U.S. fleet had just wreaked on the Japanese carrier force attacking Midway. The TBD Devastator lost control, and he struck his head on the cockpit shield when his plane smacked the ocean.

He woke up choking on salt water, still strapped into his seat. He got himself loose just before the bomber sunk, taking Lt. Jimmy Owens with it. He managed to get free a can of fresh water and the flare gun, but the rest of the emergency supplies sank with the wreckage. His right temple throbbed, dripping with blood. The salt water set his wounds on fire, but he ignored the pain. He swam clear of the sinking plane, his May West life-jacket keeping him afloat.

He relaxed his body, didn't thrash like some men did. He let the sea carry him, his old friend, a kind mother he knew growing up on the Gulf of Mexico, every morning out in a dingy fishing for flounder. He searched the horizon for any signs of the American fleet, not one tin can. The ocean flowed into the horizon, a vast highway. Her spirit felt different here, not the sea Wilbur had known: careless, without regard, a blind woman, blind eternity, caring little for the waif knotted in the folds of her skirt.

Floating in the heart of eternity, it was just Wilbur and his God.

And he knew God would not speak to him. Wilbur had killed, breaking one of the highest laws. So many had killed. God had turned his back on the world in its madness. He had granted man industry, and humans had turned this into the means to mass murder. Nothing could redeem them.

Wilbur spotted something to the west, something bobbing in the water. It might have been some gear, a bit of wreckage, anything that might help. He paddled over, trying to judge the distance.

Swimming closer, he made out the head, shoulders of another downed pilot.

"Hey buddy," he said, tugging on his shoulder. "Boy, am I glad to see you. You can't see it under water, but I'm dancing. Yes sir."

He turned him round and looked into the face of the enemy.

Propaganda films rolled before his eyes summoning distrust, revulsion, betrayal, serpents singing in his soul. Lord knows he'd killed enough of the enemy, the serpents of war spewing poison into him. On the big screen, the enemy looked larger than life, monochromatic giants whose only aim was to bring down society. Wilbur had never been so close to the enemy before. His eyes closed, face gentle like a snowfall, he appeared as a boy sleeping.

He opened his eyes, looked over Wilbur, trying to put the pieces together. The seams of his eyes split, and he thrashed in the water, pushing away from Wilbur, reaching for a sheath strapped to his chest. It was too small to be his sword, probably can't fit into the cockpit.

"Buddy. Hey. Take it easy."

In his panic, he kept sucking down water, choking. He'd drown if he kept it up.

"Tiger. I'm not going to hurt you."

He tried to calm him before he took in too much water, and finally an old instinct kicked in when he was taking care of his infant brother and his brother wouldn't stop crying. He set his words to the music of a lullaby.

"Calm down little buddy,"

"No more war for us,"

"Papa's going to buy you,"

"A shot of Kentucky bourbon."

At first, the Japanese pilot turned his head in puzzlement. He calmed, letting his arms float, choking up the last of the water. Wilbur lifted him up to keep his mouth clear of the waves.

"I reckon buddy," Wilbur told him. "Floating out here in the middle of the deep blue, dumb as shark bait, we're out of the war. So why don't we rest a spell, maybe take in some of the sights?"

The pilot half nodded, and Wilbur wondered if he understood. Words were not required. Their situation was obvious.

For the first night they just hovered there, rocking in the waves. Wilbur kept an eye out for flying boats looking for survivors. After a battle like that, it wouldn't take long to be found. Wilbur didn't mind the peace. He and his new buddy had fallen out of the war, and there were times when he could just close his eyes and be at peace.

The Japanese pilot never spoke a word, but Wilbur could read his eyes. This too brought him peace, for he did not see thorn bushes there. Peace lived in the heart of the enemy too.

They shared the little resources they had, conserving them. By the second sunrise, Wilbur's head started to crack like a boiled egg. He could see spectral nets in the clouds, angels flying low to fish.

"This is my angel, Angela," he said, taking out the photo of his wife from his top pocket. The image had begun to melt from contact with the water. He showed it to the Japanese pilot. He nodded, taking out his own photo--a woman in a kimono, her hair tied into a bun, walking along a luminous beach.

"Beautiful gal," Wilbur said.

"This one is my dad. He's a minister back home in Angleton. He was against the war, said killing was God's business. He didn't understand what we were fighting for. I can't understand it either. Think God will ever forgive us for this? I don't see how he can."

The Japanese pilot just listened, his bloodshot eyes studying the austere figure in the photo.

For the second time, the ocean swallowed the sun in the west. Wilbur's body ached. His legs had gone numb, and he kept reaching down to scratch, swearing he saw fish nibbling at them. He gave the last mouthful of fresh water to his new friend. The Japanese pilot took a small sip and returned the remainder to Wilbur. They took shifts sleeping, but by then he slumbered fitfully.

"They ain't going to find us," Wilbur said.

The sunburn on his face stung like a jellyfish.

Wilbur set Angela's picture loose on the waves, blew it a kiss.

"I'm sorry Angel," he told it. "It don't matter much now. God don't see us no more. It's better to just let go."

Wilbur worked at the straps on his lifejacket, trying to set himself loose. He'd be able to sleep at the bottom of the sea. Nice and cool down there. No more fish nibbling at his legs. He got one strap free.

The Japanese pilot grabbed Wilbur's shoulders.

"Best now to sleep. Go to sleep little doggies."

Wilbur worked at the other strap.

He took Wilbur's face, held it tight, aligning their eyes. Wilbur could see a light in there, a candle burning in the window, bringing you home in the long night. The other strap went, and the life vest peeled off his body. He held Wilbur up, keeping his mouth above the waves. He reached out and grabbed the vest before it floated far.

"We're all in the dark," Wilbur said. "All in the dark."

Wilbur struggled against his grip, but he held tight. If Wilbur sank, he'd follow.

"Just let me go, buddy. Just let go."

A flash of pain burned Wilbur's calf. Something tugged on it, and Wilbur twisted free, feeling his leg rip open. It brushed against his side. Crimson floated to the surface, clouding their little corner of the ocean.

"How did you know red was my favorite color?" Wilbur said.

The pilot drew his *Tanto* from the sheath strapped to his chest. The dawn sun set the blade afire.

Wilbur felt the shark brush along his legs, thrashing, in a frenzy from the taste of blood. The pilot handed Wilbur the life-jacket to hold onto and dove into the sea, struggling against the buoyancy of his own. The shark danced around them, single purpose pulsing through it like a machine. He couldn't see the fight in the cloudy sea. He felt a sudden jerk from the pilot, and another red cloud dispersed on the surface. He let go of the life jacket, feeling around for the shark. It slipped by, and he caught its fin. He pummeled its head, and the shark's nose broke the surface. It shut like a bear trap on the pilot's arm, and Wilbur grabbed hold of its dorsal. The shark twisted, and the pilot exacted a lethal blow. The shark released then swam on its side. It dove sideways and left their sight. They waited for it to return. They waited.

The pilot's grip never lightened on Wilbur, keeping him up, even as the pilot passed out from blood loss. Soon after, Wilbur spotted a flying boat. He opened the seal on his flare gun and fired.

They finished their tea, and Grandfather asked Keiko to clear the table. She went about her chore, feeling the bobbing of the waves from Wilbur's story. Grandfather reflected in silence.

Someone tapped the door.

"This must be them," Matthews-san said.

"More visitors?" said Keiko, trying to refrain from running to the door. She would meet many *gaijin* that day and have much to say tomorrow at school.

A young woman waited at the door, and Keiko marveled at her hair--golden like sunlight. She had a boy with her wearing a brown windbreaker, a little taller than Keiko.

"My son-in-law is stationed on Okinawa," Matthews-san said. "My daughter and grandson came with me to visit."

Grandfather bowed. Keiko showed them where to switch their shoes for slippers.

"This is my daughter, Karen. And my grandson, William Ichi Deal."

"Sorry we're late," she said. "We had to ask a policeman to help us find the house."

"I'm so pleased to meet you, Mr. Moto."

She kissed Grandfather's cheek.

"She was born a few years after the war," Wilbur said. "She wouldn't be here if it wasn't for you."

Grandfather's mouth quivered, and he sucked on his lips, maintaining his composure. He turned his head to hide his weeping, but Keiko spotted a tear streaming from his eye. The guests looked away out of politeness.

"I know how you've lost your wife and daughter, and boy did my heart ache for you. When your daughter died, I knew I had to bring my family here to meet you. Open your gift, Ichi. From your family."

Grandfather found the package, carefully opening the wrapping paper, to reveal a box of paints and brushes.

He bowed, saying, "A beautiful gift of the soul."

"I would like to call you *ojii-san* also," Karen said to Grandfather. "Did I say that right?"

Matthews-san nodded to her.

For the first time since her mother died, Keiko saw the tide come back in Grandfather's eyes.

"*Ojii-san*," said Karen. "My family still has the paintings you did when you were a P.O.W. I adore the cherry blossoms. We planted one in the yard. I always get depressed when the blossoms fall away."

"*Ojii-san*," Keiko said. "We should go to the park to see the *sakura*."

The weatherman said the *sakura* line had reached Shikoku. In early spring, the cherry blossoms would bloom in Okinawa to the south and flow like a flock of butterflies north to Hokkaido.

"Would you paint them for me?" Karen asked.

Grandfather went into his studio to fold up his easel and his bag.

"Your cherry blossoms will never die, *musume*."

Flash, Bullet Train

a poem by Nora Nadjarian

I will arrive carrying
a rice paper parcel
full of the love letters

I never sent you.

You will recognize me
by the cherry petals
falling off my hair

Across my face.

My eyes will recite
haiku about snow
and the taste of plums

Hidden in winter.

On my cold feet,
snowdrops and on the
snowdrops, my cold feet,

Achingly small and bitter.

The station will be totally empty
and white, except for a rustle
from my dark red kimono

and the breath of a bullet train
flashing past.

Birds in the Trees

a story by Suzanne Kamata

On the first day of spring, Keita Hosokawa fell in love with a bird. If anyone had told him a week before that this would happen, he wouldn't have believed it. He was fed up with birds. Specifically crows.

That year the crows seemed greater in number than ever before. Fatter, too. They feasted at the roadside shrines where hump-backed ladies set out oranges and bowls of cooked rice for their dear departed. They swooped down on cemeteries and ate the offerings from gravestones. They ate until they were as big as roosters, until it seemed as if the telephone wires would not support them.

As if there wasn't enough food available elsewhere, they fed in Keita's orchard. He could see them from the window as he ate his breakfast a murder of crows settling in the branches of his pear trees. The sight of them made him weary before the days work had even begun. He turned away from the window and tried to smile at his son.

Ichiro sat in his high chair, banging his spoon on the tray. His bib was soaked with drool. Wan wan wan! he said, barking like a dog.

Keita sighed. He tried to get the boy to say *otōsan* or even papa, which was easier to pronounce than the Japanese word for father, but he wouldn't learn. He could say mama and make a variety of animal sounds, but he seemed to willfully ignore Keita.

Papa, Keita said softly, trying once again.

Ichiro's spoon flew out of his spit-slimed hand and onto the floor. Miaow, he said, spotting Kitty in the corner.

Papa, Keita repeated.

From the kitchen, his wife Misa giggled. Don't feel so bad, she said. He doesn't see you enough to know who you are. He'll figure it out soon enough.

He doesn't see me because I'm out in the field trying to protect his legacy, Keita said, feeling suddenly angry. He knew that Ichiro wasn't to blame. He was a baby. He slept almost all of the time. When he was a little bigger, Keita would take him out into the orchard and prop him against a tree. This is all yours, he would tell him, as his own father had once taught him. Someday you'll take care of these trees.

Even if Keita and Misa had other children, Ichiro, as the firstborn son, was entitled to the family property. The land with all of its trees and the house would be passed on just as it had been for generations before.

Normally, Keita's parents were at the breakfast table with them, but they had departed the previous day for Texas to visit Keita's sister. She was a doctor, and she had gone to the United States to do research and learn the latest treatments for kidney diseases. Keita's parents worried about her because she was past thirty and as yet unmarried. It didn't matter to them that she had bought her own house and drove in an imported car, or that she could afford annual vacations to Europe. They had hopes of a traditional life for her one with a husband and kids. Still, she was allowed to do as she pleased. Keita, as the oldest son, was the one who was bound to follow their desires.

When Keita had turned twenty-nine, his mother had declared that it was time for him to take a bride. He felt the weight of duty and meekly agreed. His first choice of wife, a giggly young woman with waist-length hair and dimples, had seemed to like him but refused the role of farm wife. The next ten women he met had virtually identical reactions. They wanted to have careers in tall, air-conditioned buildings. They didn't want to share the roof with his parents. He was thinking that he might have to settle for a foreign bride, one of the Southeast Asians sent to Japan to marry the country's undesirable bachelors, and he wondered how he would be able to communicate with such a woman. He had never studied Thai or Tagalog, and his English wasn't very good.

But then his luck had changed. A family friend introduced him to Misa, a woman who had grown up on a farm. She knew all about pears how to pollinate them, how to batten the low branches when a typhoon was approaching, how to turn them into a sweet liqueur. Her hair was short, and she didn't mind getting dirt under her fingernails.

The mayor attended the wedding and made a speech praising their complementary qualities. Keita had always been a dreamy boy, he said, but Misa was of simple tastes and practical and she would keep him tethered to the earth. They honeymooned in Hawaii, where Keita marveled at the acres of pineapples and sugar cane. What it must be like to be in charge of all that! His family's farm was modest in comparison.

For the first year of their marriage, Keita and Misa had worked side by side among the trees, but then she became pregnant, and nausea and headaches had forced her to stay in the house.

On this day, Keita would be going into the field alone. Misa would play with Ichiro. Maybe she'd watch the afternoon dramas while he napped. With Keita's mother in Texas, she'd be able to relax for a change. Keita, too. The bickering women made him feel tired, made him almost want to stay in the orchard.

He scraped the last grain of rice from his bowl and pushed the breakfast dishes away. I guess I'd better get out there before the crows eat all of my fruit.

Misa murmured her agreement and then gathered up the dishes for washing.

Ichiro said, Moo!

He could hear the crows as he stomped onto the field in his work boots. Kah! Kah! They seemed to be mocking him, telling jokes at his expense.

Keita didn't know how to make them go away. He'd staked a scarecrow a straw man in a floppy hat, plaid shirt and worn-out jeans at the center of the field, but the birds didn't seem to mind. They perched on the dummy's shoulder. He'd then tied aluminum pie pans to the branches of trees, having heard that the metallic brilliance would ward off feathered intruders, but after a day or two of being wary, the crows had returned in full force.

If he'd had a gun, he would have blasted into the trees, but he had no such weapon. A sudden burst of fury sparked him with energy. He filled his lungs and screamed, Iiiiiiyyaaaa! He ran through the orchard waving his arms like a madman. The crows lifted into the air, flecking the sky with black. They circled cautiously, then one brave bird descended toward the trees again.

Keita sighed. If it wasn't crows, it was typhoons. If it wasn't weather, it was blight. He wished that he could take one season off from farming. A few months in, say, an office would refresh him.

He had been to the doctor recently to find out why he was always so tired. His body felt worn and damaged even though he was just thirty years old. His eyesight was failing, his girth expanding, his intestinal tract rebelling after every meal.

Too much stress, the doctor told him. You'll have to stop smoking and drinking, and you'd better find another job.

Keita had laughed. If only it were that simple. He had signed up for a karate class he'd reached black belt while in college hoping for physical release. But the weekly sparring matches left him breathless and sore, and he found himself being defeated by sixteen-year-old beginners.

Now, standing in the field, he thought about all the work that had to be done. He knew that he could call on the neighboring farmers to help, since his parents were out of the country, but asking them seemed like too much trouble. All he wanted to do was lie down under the trees and sleep.

Instead, he scrabbled for a stone and tossed it up at a plump black bird. Kah! The crow ruffled its feathers and fixed its beady eyes upon him, but it didn't fly away. Keita turned from the orchard, from his days work, and talked down to the river that ran along his property.

He found a broad, smooth stone, and he sat there to contemplate the water. The river gurgled and flowed, and its melody soothed him, a balm for frayed nerves. He listened and watched and succumbed to the caresses of the spring breeze on his face. It was in such a beatific state that he first saw the bird.

She rose a few meters in front of him on blue-tinged wings. He admired the long beak, the crimson breast as bright as a wedding kimono,. Her grace, the curve of her neck, made his heartbeat quicken. He had seen spindly-legged egrets and mallards in this stream, but never such a bird as this. In the deepest part of himself, he began to believe that this bird had been sent to him in this moment of difficulty to ease his pain. It was a wild idea, but he clung to it nevertheless.

He remained as still as the stone he sat upon, not wanting to spook this mysterious visitor. He watched as she dove into the water to catch a fish. The *ayu* wriggled in her beak, but she flew into a nearby tree and stunned the fish with a quick slap against the bark before gulping it down.

What kind of bird was she? And where had she come from? He would ask his friend Junji. Junji was a serious birdwatcher from way back. He had a life list of all the birds he wanted to see. Junji's vacations were always part of his quest to check off the birds on the list. He'd ventured as far away as Brazil to catch sight of a parrot in the wild. On a trip to the state of Washington he'd been lucky enough to see a bald eagle. His mind was an encyclopedia of bird lore.

Keita stayed by the river all morning watching the bird. He went back to the house for lunch, but he didn't tell Misa what he'd seen.

How did your work go? she asked him, dishing out curry over rice.

Fine, he said. He could not meet her eyes. He imagined Misa crying out in jealousy. What? she might say. You prefer her company to mine? What about your family? Ichiro? Me? But in reality, if he told her the truth she would probably chastise him for wasting the morning, not for being unfaithful.

He returned to the riverside after lunch, but the bird was no longer there. After an hour's vigil, he went back to his pear trees. That night he called Junji.

Sounds like a kingfisher, Junji said. But that's impossible. They don't live around here.

Maybe it got lost, Keita said. Or it might have escaped from a zoo.

Or maybe you need new glasses.

Keita didn't laugh. Tomorrow morning would bring his camera. He would show Junji that he wasn't dreaming.

The next day she was there, swooping through the trees on cobalt wings. He wondered if she had a nest nearby. He imagined eggs and then a flock of kingfishers to fly through his mornings.

He hid in the bushes, and when the bird settled for a moment on a black pine branch, he clicked the shutter. He used an entire roll of film. At dusk he returned to the house, reluctantly.

You're late, Misa said over her shoulder. She was in the living room, seated on the straw-mat floor with the baby.

I know. Sorry. Keita saw his dinner laid out on the table and knew that it was already cold. He sat down to eat.

In the early days of their marriage, Misa would have sat down beside him while he dined, even if she had already eaten. But now the baby took up almost all of her time. Keita could hear her singing to him now: Flying crows, why do you call? Cause on the mountainside we've seven, seven little babies with lovely round eyes.

She had the voice of a lark, but he hated that song. The crows that plagued his orchard were not pretty. They were like creatures from a nightmare. He'd heard of two schoolchildren being pecked by them. They dropped pebbles on the railroad tracks, messing up train schedules. So what if, according to legend, crows pulled the sun into the sky each day? The birds were a nuisance at best, and there was nothing lovely about their eyes.

He wanted to tell Misa to stop singing, but Ichiro began clapping his hands in delight.

The two of them were perfectly content without him. He felt that he was nothing more than a field hand or a houseboy.

When Keita developed the film a few days later, he was disappointed to find that none of the pictures had turned out. In some, the bird in flight appeared as a blur across the center of the photo. Others were underexposed or awash with light. Nevertheless, he showed them to Junji.

Could be a kingfisher, Keita's friend mused, squinting at the glossy prints. But they're usually more skittish around humans.

I was well hidden, Keita said. Or maybe he had a special affinity with the bird. Maybe she trusted him more than she did other people. This thought warmed him.

He considered telling Misa about the bird, waving the photos in front of Ichiro's face, but they had so much else to interest them their songs, their kisses, their secret games. No, he would keep the bird for himself.

Have you outwitted the crows? Misa asked the next morning.

Keita sighed. He'd covered the trees with netting, but a few of the black demons had found an opening. Those that couldn't get in had spent the morning tormenting the cat.

Crows are omnivorous, Junji had told him. They'll eat anything.

Even Kitty who slept at the foot of his futon? Well, maybe. He'd read an article in the newspaper about crows attacking baby squirrels in another town. The birds nudged the squirrels off the telephone wires and then ate them after they'd fallen to the ground. The reporter had called the birds a new type of serial killer.

Please don't speak to me about crows, Keita told his wife. He knew that she didn't really care about what went on in the orchard. She was just making conversation. He wished they had more to talk about, like in the old days before their marriage when they had been a mystery to one another.

Keita knew that there was work to be done, but on this morning he didn't even pretend. He loaded his video camera with a fresh tape and marched straight to the riverbank. Why hadn't he thought of this earlier? With a video he would be able to capture the grace of the bird as well as her delicate shape and brilliant colors.

Keita crouched in his usual spot behind a bush. The grasses there had become matted down from his daily vigils. He held his camera at the ready for an hour and then two, but the bird his bird never showed. The crows, he thought, his stomach sickening. The crows have murdered my lovely bird. If they were brave enough to dive at humans and hungry enough to eat squirrels, then wouldn't they attack smaller birds as well? He tried to muster hope, but after five hours, he left the riverbank and returned to the house.

As usual, dinner was on the table, but Keita ignored the grilled fish and soup. He poured himself a cup of chilled sake and took a big gulp.

What is it? Misa asked, the baby on her lap. She had a rattle in one hand, and she reminded Keita of a court jester. There was no way she would ever be able to understand his sorrow.

In his dreams that night the kingfisher glided on air, circling ever closer to Keita's hiding place. He sat transfixed. The bird, no bigger than a swallow, landed on his palm. She studied him with curious brown eyes and let him stroke her blue back with one finger. And then she ruffled her feathers and flew off into the sky.

Keita woke with a kernel of hope nestled in his heart. Today she would be there, waiting in the trees. He was sure of it as he bolted out the door without eating any breakfast. More than food, more than air, he needed a glimpse of his beautiful bird.

The sun rose higher in the sky as he stared at the river. The fish swam, undisturbed. Sparrows fluttered past, but there was no flash of blue. No long-beaked lover roosting on his palm. And then he heard a crack of twigs and saw the grasses twitch and part and there was Kitty, with a gift in her mouth. Keita stared in horror, not wanting to believe he had shared his bed with this animal.

His eyes filled with tears. He took off his glasses, and the bird deposited at his feet by Kitty became as blurry as it appeared in the failed photos. The cat rubbed against his legs, and he kicked her away. For so long there had been nothing bright in his life, and then when this wonder appeared, he had found joy. Yet he couldn't protect this wild thing from danger. And he couldn't protect his orchard the trees that he had been entrusted with, that he was meant to maintain for Ichiro and all the generations to follow.

He thought of the flatbed truck parked in front of his house, the one that carried the pears to market. What if he got behind the wheel and started driving? He'd leave all this behind, cross the Akashi Bridge and go as far as he could. They'd all be better off without him.

He crouched there, behind the bushes, and tired to rock the sudden loneliness out of his body. His grief was so absorbing that he didn't hear the bird calls at first.

Kah! Kah!

He looked over his shoulder and saw a black-headed figure flapping its wings. It was coming closer and closer, but he wasn't afraid. Beside it, a taller creature picked through the grasses on elegant long legs, its pure white plumage dazzling in the sunlight.

We brought you breakfast, a voice called out. You didn't eat. You must be famished.

Keita rubbed the tears from his eyes and put his glasses back on. Yes, he was hungry. He flew to meet them, his wife and his child.

Rite of Spring

flash fiction by Oonah V. Joslin

It's spring here now and cherry blossom time. My grandmother would arrange sprigs in a tall, thin vase. Three sprigs; just three, like haiku she used to say. Three is the proper number for serenity.

And she would cook *ohagi*, real *wa-gashi* not *yo-gashi*. She disapproved of western treats. I couldn't wait until the rice had cooked. I watched its steam ghost from the cooker and watched her beat the soft rice to a pulp and I dipped a licked finger, whenever I could reach, into each waiting bowl; the sweet azuli bean paste, the sugary crushed walnuts and the ground black sesame and *kinako*. Then when the rice had cooled, she'd wet my hands and show me how to form the oval balls and coat them. Always at the end, a little one for the cooks.

The cherry trees will not blossom here this spring. There is no house here now to clean for *higan*. And as I pray for the souls of my ancestors and for all the other souls departed from this place, I am so thankful that my grandmother did not witness this. I place fresh flowers on the ground and some strong green tea. "Grandmother," I say, "there are only three of us left in the family now. But don't worry. See, I've remembered the sprigs. And three is the proper number for serenity."

Schoolgirls and Salarymen

Something For Hanako
a story by Vesna McMaster

Keep steady. One foot after the other. Off the bus, up the hill. Made it this far now, no sitting down. I feel sick. Nearly there. Come on now... keys. Yes, keys. Oh, no, not dropping them. What a noise.

The door opens violently from the inside and there's Hanako. I can almost see the steam coming from her ears and little horns poking out of her hair.

"What the hell time do you call this?"

"3:42 a.m." I daren't look up as I take my shoes off at the door and try to set them neatly.

"Drinking again!"

"Hana, you know I don't like it. Have mercy."

"Hmph!"

Mercy seems in short supply. She's already in the kitchen, I can still see her from the entrance. Not a very big flat, ours. There are the dreaded plates and bowls with cling wrap over the top.

"I suppose you ate out again."

"Boss wanted *yakitori*. I couldn't say no."

"Did everyone go?"

"Almost everyone. Yamada and Nakano stayed back to finish a report." They're probably still there now, truth be told.

Hanako picks up the plate, rips off the cling film and scrapes rice and fish dramatically into the bin.

"We can't afford to waste food. We can't afford for you to go out drinking and eating."

"I know, sweet, but what can I do?"

Another snort of derision. She packs up the bin bag and shoves it at me without a glance.

"Make yourself useful and take this out before it starts stinking. Enough stench coming from you."

I take the bag and slink out.

The bins are at the back. Our block of flats is up on the hill, and backs onto pines and scrub.

As I lift the bin lid, something flashes from the bushes. Yellow, winking. The lights come forward and I see they're the eyes of a *tanuki*. He looks up at me and sniffs.

Tanuki! They live round here but you don't see them very often. Racoon dogs. Tricksters, conmen and shape shifters of the animal world.

Huh. Doesn't seem very afraid. I put the lid down quietly. My grilled fish dinner's sitting just there, so I reach in and lift the fillet out. He shuffles forward, a mass of brown and black fur.

"Here."

When I drop a piece between us, he doesn't hesitate. Two bites and it's gone. Then he looks up and gives a small whiney growl.

He eats the whole fish.

"That's it, buddy." I stand up and re-close the bag.

"Grhhgh."

One could almost fancy he gives a little bow as he turns round and vanishes back into the undergrowth.

As I turn back to the flats, I notice something at my feet, and pick it up. It's a raggedy old paper purse. A jumble of dried leaves spills out when I open it.

For what reason I know not, I put it in my pocket.

Hanako's calmed down a little, but it's still no time to tell her that tomorrow will be even worse. A big contract's due to be signed and the boss has promised to take us all out drinking to celebrate. Oh joy.

I put a hand on her shoulder instead.

"Boss was asking after you, you know."

She looks round, slightly alarmed.

"What for?"

"Oh, he was mentioning that Christmas party. You talked to him a little when you came to pick me up."

Hanako frowns. "Yes, that was a pretty bad night."

"No, no, I mean, he says he remembers what a nice-looking woman you are."

"Really?" She looks at me incredulously. As well she might: it's a total fabrication.

"Uh huh. Was going on about how he wishes his wife were more like you." Hanako's looking cheerier by the second so I carry on. "Says she's getting fat and boring and only cares about shopping."

"Huh." She twists a piece of hair behind her ear, the way she does when she's being coy. I'm lying but it doesn't matter, they'll never meet and if they do it's not something she's likely to bring up. I take the opportunity to give her a hug and a quick kiss. It seems to wake her up.

"Well, that's as may be but you smell. I don't care what time it is, take a bath before you come to bed."

It's nine o'clock the next evening and we're just out of work. Standing outside the *izakaya*, and noises and smells are spilling out of the door towards us.

Then I notice a young man standing in the glow of the red lantern outside. He looks strangely familiar. Staring straight at me, he tilts his head on one side.

"You don't want to go, do you?"

"What?" It takes a moment to realise he's addressing me.

"Do you want me to go instead of you?" He steps forward, smiling.

"Instead of me?"

"Just give me the purse I left you yesterday," he says.

Staring till my eyeballs feel dry, I take the paper purse out of my pocket. Why I'd brought it to work is a mystery. Wordless, I hand it over.

I stare even harder as he opens it, and all of a sudden it's a shining Gucci wallet, stuffed with crisp wads of money.

"I'll take the boss for a merry spin," he whispers in my ear, winking with a yellow glint.

As I watch, he moves towards the boss and bows, leading the way in. The boss greets him by my name, and indeed the young man looks exactly like me now. As I stand open-mouthed, the whole company melts into the building to drink the night away.

It's not even ten o'clock and I'm nearly home. On the walk back from the bus stop, I see three full red peonies hanging over a garden wall, and filch them. They're dripping with dew as I tear the stalks silently. Not quite closed for the night.

Something for Hanako.

Kibou

a story by Simon Paul Wilson

My mother says the same thing every Sunday as I sit by the door and put on my shoes.

"You are not leaving the house looking like that!"

I am a huge fan of GothLoli, so I kind of understand why she nags me so much. That day, however, I was dressed in a sedate ensemble consisting of a white school blouse, red tie, red and green plaid skirt, black knee-socks and some rather sensible black pumps.

On reflection, perhaps my skirt was a little on the short side, but still….

As I checked my backpack to make sure I had everything I needed for a day out cruising Takeshita Street, my mother continued, "When I was your age…"

Blah, blah, blah.

I gave her a sly wink and said I would be willing to change into a Kimono if she thought that was more acceptable.

"Now, there is no need for your cheek!" she spluttered. "I am going to have some serious words with—"

And then she was gone.

Just like that.

One minute she was there and the next she wasn't.

I checked around the house to see if I could find her in another room. My search drew a blank, and added my father to the missing persons list.

Many people would have been freaking out by this point, but I remained calm about the whole thing. The bizarreness of the situation just didn't press my panic button. I sat down on the sofa for a few minutes and wracked my brains to find a rational explanation for their mysterious vanishing act.

The first thing that popped into my head was the possibility that my parents had been abducted by aliens.

I ran outside to see if there was a huge spaceship hovering above our house. There wasn't. Either I could rule out aliens as a possible cause or my parents were already light-years away and heading for an unknown world in a strange and far-away galaxy.

I was about to go back inside when I was struck by how quiet it was. I looked up and down the street and saw no one: no children playing in gardens or riding bicycles; no cars being washed, or filled with families setting off for a day-trip somewhere; no joggers keen to take advantage of the crisp morning air. No one.

There was not a single trace of human life to be seen.

I decided to check the Yamamoto's place across the road. After hammering on the door for several minutes and getting no reply, I gave up and went to the Murakami's. Their front door was open a fraction, so I pushed it open further and politely asked if anyone was home. No reply came from within. I closed the door and returned to my own empty house.

I searched the internet for any news or gossip to do with sudden mass disappearances and came up empty-handed. I logged on to various chat rooms and messaging services, but found I was the only person online. The phone lines seemed to work, but none of my friends or family would pick-up; no one I knew in Tokyo, Osaka or Kyoto answered. I turned on the TV. Channel after channel was white noise and static; the radio had a similar tale to tell.

Hopelessness crept over me. I had no idea what to do and no one to turn to for advice. All evidence pointed toward me being the only person left in the world.

I shuffled around the house like a zombie until my stomach started to ache due to lack of food. I sat at the kitchen table and ate six soda crackers, a piece of chocolate cake and drank two cans of cola. Then I shuffled around the house some more.

Later that afternoon, a thought struck me; seeing as everyone had suddenly vanished at the same time, maybe there was a chance they would all magically reappear at some point. With this in mind, I decided it may be a good idea to carry on as normal.

It was too late in the day to head out to Harajuku and the thought of being the only living person in the middle of a deserted and lifeless Tokyo gave me the creeps, so I opted for staying put and waiting for everyone to eventually return.

I spent the rest of the afternoon and early evening curled up on the sofa listening to the stereo. Outside the sky slowly changed from blue to red as the sun started to set and night began its steady approach. As I watched the sun gradually fade away, I wondered if I was sharing this view with anyone else.

The darkness outside was absolute. Eerie stillness filled the house. I had seen too many films on the end of the world and didn't fancy my house being besieged by vampires or zombies intent on tearing me limb from limb, but the idea of staying in a totally dark house was not one I wanted to entertain.

I turned the volume up on the stereo by several notches and went around the house switching on every light. If there was anyone else out there, maybe turning my house into a beacon for all to see would be a good way to reconnect with the living world. Although I had only been on my own for about ten hours, I had started to crave human company.

There was also a chance that there was something lurking in the dark that was less than friendly, so with this in mind, I locked every door and window to be on the safe side.

I knew my over-active imagination was getting the better of me. The idea of the undead roaming the streets in search of fresh brains to feast upon was just as ridiculous as believing the whole of mankind could be erased from existence in the blink of an eye.

Except that's exactly what had happened.

I did rule out becoming the target of vengeful ghosts. I mean, I had done nothing wrong. Why on earth would ghosts come after me? It wasn't my fault that everyone had vanished, was it? As far as I could tell, I was the victim in this scenario. I had been abandoned, left alone in an empty world.

Hell, they all owed me an apology, if anything!

I was very hungry, so I cooked some noodles with some strips of beef and peppers. My stomach growled while I prepared my meal, but my appetite faded after only a few mouthfuls. I put what I couldn't eat into the fridge and went back to the sofa and promptly fell asleep.

The next morning, a heavy rain descended from the heavens. Sadly, this new day did not see the return of the human race.

I sat by the living-room window for most of the day and watched the storm. Drops of rain the size of duck eggs bombarded the window as the silent streets were transformed into rivers. I looked up at the sky and saw nothing but angry black clouds. It was like the Earth was cleaning itself after finally getting rid of the cause of all its troubles, scrubbing away furiously until its surface would sparkle and gleam in the light of the sun with mankind just a memory best forgotten.

A deep sense of melancholy struck me as I watched the storm rage and I realised that I was probably the only person watching such an exhibition of savage beauty.

Why had Mother Earth forgotten me?

Was she finally sick of man polluting and exploiting her? If she had decided to get shot of her burden, then why had I been left behind? Did she have other plans for me? Was it her intention that I should start the human race anew? If that was the case, then there had to be someone else alive out there, as repopulating the planet was a job for two at least.

I was unsure I wanted such a huge responsibility. A task of that magnitude was a lot to put on the shoulders of a girl who was only just approaching sixteen.

I sighed deeply and leaned my head against the cold glass; tears ran down my face as the water outside raced along the streets.

The rain did not stop all day. I returned to pacing around the house without direction or purpose. I tried once more to eat the meal I had cooked the previous day and found that my appetite had also been snatched away by unknown forces.

Returning to the sofa, I realised that if hunger didn't kill me, then boredom surely would.

I awoke the next morning to find that the rain had stopped at long last. I peered out of the window to see the sun had reclaimed mastery of a sky so blue it almost left me breathless.

After going around the house and turning off all the lights, I returned to the living-room to see a large black cat with its face pressed against the window.

Excited to have company at last, I hurried to the window to let it in. The cat mouthed several equally ecstatic but silent meows. As soon as the window was open, the cat leapt into the room and dashed into the kitchen with its tail held high, purring happily.

I followed my new companion and found it sitting and gazing up at the fridge.

"Are you hungry?"

The cat gave a loud meow to confirm that it was.

"Me too," I said, feeling my appetite finally return.

I placed the bowl of beef strips and peppers in front of my feline guest and watched as he tucked in with relish,

"Taste good?" I asked. The cat gave no audible reply, but I could see by the way he was demolishing the meal that it was an affirmative.

Looking through the contents of the fridge, I found some pork, bean sprouts and mushrooms that still looked and smelled fresh so I decided to stir-fry them with some noodles. As I was preparing the food, the cat leapt onto the kitchen work surface to observe what I was doing. I looked back to his bowl to see it was spotlessly clean.

"It was that good? Or were you just really hungry?"

The cat purred and started to clean itself. I took that as a yes to both.

I shared my meal with my new friend. It felt good to be able to be in the presence of another living creature, even though the cat could offer little in the way of conversation.

The cat left me to my own devices as I cleaned and tidied the kitchen. Upon returning to the living room, I found it curled up and fast asleep on the sofa. I stood and watched for a while as it peacefully slumbered, carefree and content.

There were plenty of cats in the neighborhood, but I had never seen this particular one before. Judging by its appearance, it looked as if it had been well cared for: its black coat was shiny and thick, which showed that the cat was both young and healthy. There was no collar to show signs of ownership or its name though.

"Do you have a name?" I asked.

The cat's left paw twitched twice.

"Is that once for yes and twice for no?"

The cat did not respond.

"Well, if we are going to be friends, you are going to need a name." I informed my sleeping friend. "Now, are you a boy or girl?"

No answer.

"I think you are a boy. I mean, you are quite a big cat, so I reckon I am right."

No comment.

"OK. Well, if you don't mind, I am going to call you Kibou. Is that OK with you, Kibou?"

Kibou remained silent.

"Cool. Kibou it is. OK, Kibou. I am going to go upstairs to have a shower. When I come back we can have a nice long chat. OK?"

His right ear twitched once. I took that as a yes.

As I stood naked in the steam-filled bathroom, it dawned on me that I had not heard or seen any animals since all the people disappeared. Not one bird singing in the trees, not one dog barking for food or attention. Nothing.

Had Mother Earth gotten sick of all life?

I could kind of understand her anger with us, but what had cats and dogs ever done?

Were goldfish evil? Were elephants a constant annoyance? What possible reason could she have for hating dolphins?

None of it seemed to make any sense. Not only had I slipped her mind but so had poor Kibou. What had he done to deserve the same fate as me?

After showering, I cleaned my teeth, brushed my hair and changed into a pair of black jeans and a red hooded sweater. Feeling clean and refreshed, I went back downstairs to spend time with the last remaining cat in existence.

I spent over an hour talking to Kibou about what had happened and my opinions on the subject. Kibou turned out to be a great listener but didn't have many thoughts of his own. Occasionally his right ear would twitch or he gave a soft purr, seemingly content to just curl up on my lap and listen to what I had to say.

When I ran out of things to discuss, I closed my eyes and drifted into a deep and restful sleep.

The room was pitch-black when I woke up.

My phone was ringing.

I shot up out of the chair, forgetting that Kibou was on my lap. He gave a startled meow as he leapt away from me and disappeared into the darkness.

I raced towards the front door where my bag was. I felt for the light switch in the hall and flicked it on; the sudden burst of fluorescent light dazzled me. I blinked my eyes several times in an attempt to regain my sight.

"Please don't hang up."

My phone continued to ring. I fell to my knees, grabbed my bag and frantically unzipped the side pocket.

"Please don't hang up. Please don't hang up."

I pulled the phone out of the pocket in a shower of tissues and loose change.

"PLEASE DON'T HANG UP!"

The phone was vibrating madly in my shaking hand. I pressed accept call and jammed it against my ear.

"Please don't hang up. I'm here, I'm here. Please don't hang up! Please." My eyes began to fill with tears.

Silence.

The tears began to stream down my face as I broke down and started sobbing into the phone: "Please talk to me. Please don't leave me all alone. Please."

Silence.

"Please…."

"Are you ready?" said a voice.

A person's voice.

A boy's voice.

My tears instantly turned from sadness to joy. My whole being was filled with elation. I was talking to someone.

I was not alone.

"Hello. My name is Miho. I am so happy to hear your voice. Thank you. Thank you for finding me. Thank you. My name is Miho. I'm alive. Please don't hang up."

"Are you ready?"

I wiped my eyes on the back of my sleeve and attempted to regain composure.

"Ready for what?" I asked.

"Ready to leave."

"Leave?"

"Yes. Are you ready? I will be coming to collect you shortly."

I was confused, not to mention a little scared. The voice at the other end of the line definitely belonged to a boy. I guessed it was someone close to my age, as he sounded a little like one of my male classmates, but the way he spoke was cold and clipped.

He didn't seem to be as excited as I was to know that there were now at least two people inhabiting the Earth.

I coughed nervously and asked him for his name.

"Are names important?" He sounded genuinely puzzled.

"Of course they are!"

"Really?"

"Yes!"

"Hmmm." The boy remained silent for a few seconds. "OK, you can call me Kibou."

I was unsure if I had heard him correctly, so I asked him to repeat what he had just said.

"You can call me Kibou."

When I failed to respond, Kibou the Boy asked if I was OK.

"Yes, I'm fine." I lied.

"Is there something wrong with my name?" He sounded a little hurt and I couldn't help but feel a pang of guilt.

"No, nothing wrong at all," I apologized. "It's just that it's a bit of a coincidence."

"How is it a coincidence?"

"Well, I found a cat today and named him Kibou."

"You found a cat today?"

"Actually he found me."

"And his name is Kibou?"

"It is now. I have no idea what his name was before, but I thought Kibou kind of suited him."

Kibou the Cat appeared and sat next to me, purring as if to say he had heard me talking about him. I stroked his head and waited for Kibou the Boy to continue the conversation. After two or three minutes of silence, I began to wonder if he was still at the other end of the line.

"Are you still there?"

"Yes. I am here."

"OK," I said, slightly relieved. "I thought you had gone."

"No, I am still here. But I will have to go soon."

"Where are you going?"

"I am coming to collect you. Are you ready to go?"

A sudden wave of cold engulfed my body and I shivered violently. "What do you mean? Where are you taking me?"

Kibou the Boy remained silent.

"Hello? Are you there?"

Nothing.

The feeling of cold gave way to panic as fresh tears started to flow.

"Please. Are you there? I don't understand what you mean. I am so alone. Don't leave me now. I don't understand what has happened. I don't understand what is happening to me. Why was I forgotten? Why did everyone leave me?

Please. Please help me.

Please…."

With the phone cradled against my ear, I sat by the front door of my house and cried until every last tear was spent and there was nothing left but sound.

"I am sorry you were forgotten."

I was unable to speak; sorrow had taken absolute control of my body. All I could do was listen as Kibou the Boy spoke to me, his voice now warm and soothing.

"I understand you are hurting, Miho. I know you feel so alone right now, that you are confused and scared and I am sorry.

I am so very sorry.

But I want you to know, Miho, that you are also very brave.

You should feel proud of yourself. You never gave up on waiting. You held onto hope. That is how I found you. Now I can come and collect you and take you to where you ought to be.

There are so many people here, Miho. You will never feel lonely again, I promise you."

I wiped my face on my tear-soaked sleeve and took several deep breaths.

"Are my parents and friends there?"

"I cannot say right now, but I know they will be here soon."

"Can I bring Kibou?"

"Of course you can. I am going to come to collect both of you."

Kibou the Cat climbed onto my lap and gave a loud meow. I took the phone away from my ear for a moment and stroked his head.

"Do you think we should go?"

His right ear twitched once.

I returned the phone to my ear.

"We're ready."

"I am happy to hear that, Miho. Just stay where you are and I will come and collect you very soon."

"OK. See you soon."

There was no reply, he had already gone.

He was coming to collect me.

To collect us.

Kibou was already asleep in my lap. I stroked his soft fur and asked him if he thought his namesake would arrive soon; one twitch from his right ear was his reply.

"I hope so, Kibou. I hope so."

I rested my head against the wall and closed my eyes.

two haiku
by Anonymous

anime fangirls

with pink plastic hair

sing in private booths

manga in briefcase

with H scenes in love hotels

perfect politeness

Geisha by Kruti Kothari
(charcoal painting)

Worm House

flash fiction by Vaishali Shroff

She waved good bye as she left for school, trying to manage her raincoat hood and blue umbrella -- her own little sky, as she'd always quip. Her tiny shoulders bearing the weight of her school bag and this world.

I watched from the window as she sneaked a peek through her umbrella to enjoy the drizzle. The raindrops gleamed like dew on her face as the sun played peek-a-boo.

She enjoyed a little jig in the air, swirling the umbrella with both hands and her boots in the air! But the very next moment I saw her stop, look down, and stoop on the ground. She fixed her gaze at something in a puddle. Her face seemed so restless. Like an impatient sun trying to chase away a wandering cloud.

"A worm!" she exclaimed, "It will drown!"

She looked around for help and gave up; perhaps looking for a fallen leaf in a concrete jungle where tall trees have been replaced by high rises and shrubs that lined the sides of the road have been replaced by garbage bins and decorative, concrete fountains that seldom seem to work. She quickly got her bag off her back, opened it, and tore a sheet of paper from her book. She folded it in half and then folded it again. Opened and folded it back again till it was perfect at the edges and seams.

I wondered what she did and what she was trying to do. She reminded me of her father who tore sheets from his science journals to make paper rockets and throw them at me during our lectures in college.

The paper folding looked so intricate, yet she had an it's-no-rocket-science look on her face. But it seemed a lot like how we live -- tread on roads that excite us, realize we are not meant for the roads or the roads are not meant for us. Take a different road, wonder where it'll lead, hoping it will lead to where we want it to lead, till we reach the countryside that lives in a corner of our dreams and say aha!

The folding continued till she broke into a smile and held a beautiful little paper boat. She quickly got a pen and scribbled "Worm House" on its side before setting it afloat where the worm squirmed. The smile grew wider as the worm wiggled its way up and into the boat. Then she got up, having done her job, having given the worm a home.

She enjoyed a little jig in the air, swirling the umbrella with both hands, and boots in the air!

Dusting her hands and skirt, her bag back on her tiny shoulders, there she was, smiling, walking towards school. A little wet, a little late.

Junko's Smile
a story by Liz Haigh

If you'd told me a month ago that I'd be so excited about going to a Hanami, I wouldn't have believed you. I didn't go to any parties at all in the Cherry Blossom season last year. My parents begged me to go out with them. But I defiantly said, "No" and stayed home alone in my room, which seemed the right thing to do for a boy of sixteen.

This year, I couldn't wait. Not because I was going to a party with my parents, but because I was going to a party with Meiko, the hottest girl in high school. That's not strictly true; I wasn't going with her - I mean it was her party and I was invited - which is nearly the same thing. Technically, she had a boyfriend - Riku Shibata, he was the school baseball ace. Sure, he was good looking but not that clever. I thought it would only be a matter of time until she tired of him. That's what I told my friends Akio and Daichi as we walked home from school on the Friday before the party. They both fell about laughing, but I told them I'd be the one laughing when I rolled up at school on Monday and announced Meiko was now mine. My plan to win her over involved my arriving at the party with a large box of pizza and some cold beers. I once overheard Meiko say she loved Spicy Italiano.

I got up early on the day of the party and took a very long shower in preparation for the long evening ahead. As the day dragged on and I got hot waiting for the hours to pass, I decided I'd better take another shower before finally getting dressed into my going out clothes.

I had ten thousand yen in my pocket all ready to call in at Domino's Pizza on my way to the party. Everything was going according to plan until I walked into the kitchen. My father was reading his paper in the corner while my mother was packing a very large amount of sushi into a box.

"You look smart Kazuo," she said smiling. "Look I have made a nice big box of sushi for you to take to the party."

"Oh don't worry about it Mother, I am planning to buy some pizza and cold b..." Luckily I just stopped myself in time from saying I was going to take cold beer to the party but it seemed the damage had already done with the word, "pizza."

My mother's face dropped and her eyes took on the sadness a child has when she's lost her kitten.

"Pizza," my father spat. "Pizza is not a suitable food to take to a Hanami. You have our family name to consider. And your mother has worked hard all day preparing this sushi. You don't realise what a lucky boy you are."

A year ago, I would probably have stormed to my room at this point, not coming out for hours and have completely missed the party. As I was getting older, I was also getting wiser.

"I am so sorry Father. I will take the sushi to the party. Thank you, mother for making it. I'm sure everyone will really enjoy it."

I then left as quickly as possible, taking care to correctly carry the box of sushi under my arm. My plan was to stash the sushi under a bush as soon as I was a safe distance from the house, then go buy some pizza.

I was so busy thinking about the party, planning what I was going to say to Meiko when I arrived, that I'd almost reached the park still holding my box of sushi. Meiko's party was going to be under the cherry blossom tree in the far left hand corner. The one a bit out of the way. Her older brother was going to get there early with his mates and reserve it for us.

I was just about to launch my hoard of sushi and run across the road to Domino's Pizza, when I almost stumbled over a girl kneeling on the pavement. All around her was a squashed box and bits of rice, fish and seaweed.

"Are you okay?" I asked as I knelt down to see if I could help.

"I tripped up and I've dropped all the sushi," she said.

Then I realised I knew the girl. It was Junko from my science class. I hadn't recognised her straight away. In school she always wore her hair in two tight pigtails, making her look rather serious and studious. This evening she wore her hair down with a white flower pinned on the left hand side. Her face looked softer with her hair down; she looked different, somehow vulnerable. I felt a strange fluttering in my chest as I looked at her. Maybe I was hungry.

"Are you hurt?" I asked.

"No, I'm fine but my sister and I worked all afternoon making this sushi. Now I've ruined it and have nothing to take to the party." She was wearing a beautiful powder blue dress, this combined with the flower in her hair made her outfit look so cheerful, but in sharp contrast with her eyes cast down her face looked so sad.

"Please don't worry. Here look I have a big box of sushi here which my mother made. I'd really like you to take it."

My most generous offer of the sushi which I was planning to trash anyway, was rewarded by the most beautiful smile I'd ever seen.

"I couldn't possibly take it. What will you take? She asked.

"We could carry it in to the park together," I suggested.

"That would be wonderful."

I helped Junko to her feet. She fretted that she had dirtied her beautiful dress. I told her she looked just fine and she blushed.

As we walked into the park I started to make my way to the left but Junko pulled right.

"The party is over here," she said.

"Aren't you going to Meiko's party?" I asked.

"Oh you are a lucky boy; no I'm not going there; I wasn't invited. I'm going to the community party over there. My uncle has organised it, anyone can go along. But if you are going to Meiko's you must take the sushi there."

"No I insist you take it," I said.

Junko's head tilted gently to one side and her face took on that lost vulnerable look again.

"Will you come with me for a short while? I'd like you to meet my sister and help me explain how I dropped our sushi."

"Okay, I will," I said smiling. I could always nip out of the park and pick up some pizza and arrive late at Meiko's party; it would probably be cool to arrive not on time.

As we approached the party, there was quite a big crowd there already, people of all different ages, many had put down blankets and chairs and there was already a feast of food and drink laid out. The first person we met was Junko's uncle. He was under the largest tree in the centre of the park. The tree's boughs were heavily laden with cherry blossom making a soft pink canopy for the party.

Junko introduced me, "This is Kazuo from my school. He has very generously given us this huge box of sushi which his mother has prepared."

"You are most welcome Kazuo. Please sit down and have a drink." Sitting under the cherry tree I watched Junko as she opened up my mother's box and began offering it to the other guests.

Junko's uncle tried some of my mother's *Temaki*, which is one of her specialities; she rolls the rice, seaweed, the fish and her own home-made pickles into a perfect tight cone.

"This is very fine sushi, Kazuo. You're mother is a very good cook. You are a very lucky boy"

As I sat under the cherry tree, a gentle breeze came through causing some blossom petals to gently rain down on us. Some had landed in Junko's hair. She caught me looking at her and smiled. I smiled back and for the first time in my life I realised, yes I was a very lucky boy.

Kimika and the Ants

flash fiction by D.R.D. Bruton

Kimika stares at the numbers she has set down on the page, sees them running all ways, like ants across the paper, and she chases those ants with her pen, never quite catching them. Kimika does not understand what her teacher, Mr Osaka, has told her to do, cannot remember the rules to make those numbers sit still. She can see the other girls in the class, bent over their work, their small-moon faces crumpled and creased with concentration, and they are writing. Kimika can hear the scritch scratch of their pens, and she thinks she is the only one who sees ants.

Kimika thinks of Grandpa Ishio and the stories in his head. She thinks of the biggest number in the world; she cannot yet put a name to that number but she thinks it must be more than a hundred and that is the number of the stories that her Grandpa Ishio has. She remembers those stories, though sometimes in her head they are just one story. She wishes Grandpa Ishio was with her now; he would have the words to stop those ants from running this way and that, for there is a magic in words, Grandpa Ishio says.

Kimika makes a story come, one of Grandpa Ishio's stories. It is the one about the boy who emerged full formed from the great peach stone and he grew as quick as stories can and came to be the warrior Momotaro. Kimika tells herself of the Lord Monkey and the Lord Brindled Dog and the Lord Pheasant of the Moor, and how they sailed with Momotaro out across the sea in a bamboo boat and, reaching a far off island, they found and thrashed the great ogres that were the terror of the country, and they afterwards brought back all the lost treasures of Japan. There were precious jewels, and coral fans, and amber beads, and emerald necklaces, and gold and silver bells, and tortoiseshell combs, and bolts of the finest silk. And there was a coat made of rice grass and wearing it made a person invisible. Kimika looks up at the clock on the wall and even those numbers are become ants. She wishes for the rice grass coat then.

"Don't forget the hammer," she says, only the voice in her head when she says it sounds like Grandpa Ishio. "Don't forget the hammer." He means the hammer that Momotaro brought back from the Isle of Ogres. And it was a magic hammer and every blow of the hammer struck showers of gold. Kimika looks down at the page of her book and she thinks that to make gold out of the ants on her page would be a fine thing indeed, and the ogre, Mr Osaka, would be pleased with that and not notice that her numbers didn't add up. Instead she scribbles with her pen.

Kimika is busy with her scribbling, not really knowing what she does, making a cloud that glowers and glowers across the whole page, and all those ants are soon shrunk to one that sits in a small white space in the middle of the paper.

"The pen is mightier than the sword," her Grandpa Ishio says with some satisfaction, and Kimika did not think that could be true till now, till she sees the one small ant trapped in the crowded darkness of her scribbling, outnumbered by the marks she has made on the page, over and over, too many to count, more than all the stories in Grandpa Ishio's head.

Mr Osaka looks up for a moment and seems to be listening to the scritch scratch music of the girls' pens, and Kimika pretends she is thinking hard, wears a mask that makes her look like all the other girls in the class. Then Kimika bends to her work and scribbles the last remaining ant into dark.

Buttons

a story by Vesna McMaster

Her foot slipped and she started to fall. Arms already full of papers, Makiko clutched them tighter as she wobbled.

"Shall we stop for an iced tea on the way?" Makiko's looking at me eagerly as she asks. Her idea of heaven is a stop at a café on an after-school Friday comic-book jaunt. Sometimes she'll even have a little cake.

"Must we?" I say. All the little corners in her round face take a sudden dive earthwards. "Oh, all right."

The bus lurches, and we both cling to the rails. The schoolbag on my back tries to topple me, and as I resist I feel the little 'pop pop' along the sailor-suit uniform's neck-line. I curse under my breath, and Makiko looks quizzical.

"These bloody outfits, they're designed by perverts. Poppers for the neck-line, poppers for the cuffs, one tug and the whole thing comes undone. Haven't they heard of stitching?"

"I think," she offers hesitantly, "It's because they have to be dry-cleaned." She holds onto my bag meekly as I re-attach the collar.

Trust her to plummet, just at the right time, the right place. She had no idea anyone else was there.

At the café we sip tea as I gently kick at the pile of satchels, gym bags, book bags and lunch bags beneath the table.

"I think he looked at me today," she says.

"Oh, good."

"I'm going to ask him."

"You've been saying that since Christmas. It's June."

"I'm nervous, OK?" Makiko runs fingers along her teacup in a pattering little racing line. I regard her unsympathetically. She avoids my gaze.

"Why don't you at least pick someone more worthwhile to moon over? That little runt. Nothing that short should ever look that smug."

"I'll never change my mind! I love him!"

"Do you think he knows yet, then?" She looks silently petrified.

"Well, you do want him to find out, eventually, don't you?" She sighs, and looks deep into her teacup. I carry on, remorseless.

"You knit him a scarf for Christmas, and deposit it in his shoebox anonymously. For Valentine's you send him a card and chocolates, and he sends you nothing in return on White Day the next month. You send him another mystery card for his birthday, and still he says nothing."

The lecture's not having the desired effect, because she's smiling more and more. It's probably the mere pleasure of reliving the experiences. I give up and drain my cup. "Come on, let's get a move on."

The chair tipped over into a final incline of no return. Makiko's eyes widened into full almonds.

She's been meaning to hint to Eisuke (the runt) that she'd like his... second button. All this time, and quite literally, not even a button.

It's a tradition, you see. If you like a girl, you can give her the second button from your school uniform. Boys who have "lost" the button seem to have that extra swagger as they flout the school dress rules. Mind you, I really wonder whether some of them have just yanked theirs off and hidden them somewhere. Can't imagine anyone accepting their buttons.

Runt he may be, but Eisuke seems a fixed constellation in Makiko's universe, obscured neither by clouds nor brighter lights.

We sit on the bus home, each reading our new comics. She looks up from hers.

"How did you get the gathering on your sleeves to line up properly?" She's blinking at me as if it's a mathematical theorem. We've been making a pair of pyjamas in Home Economics class for the last three months.

"Dunno." A vision of the hated project presents itself. Truth to tell, the gathering on my sleeves is far from even. It stands out in lumps.

"But you've finished the whole top. No-one else has. You must know how."

I put down my comic. "Maki-chan, I've finished it because I don't care. The teacher lets me read my book as long as I'm up to the class target. I just don't bother with all the basting and marking."

"But I need to know how to do good gathering. I want to make him a keepsake bag for some cookies."

"Cookies?"

"Yes, I've been practicing white chocolate ones for ages. I'm getting really good." She smiles up at me. "I know he likes white chocolate."

What the hell's wrong with cellophane. She needs help.

"They'll be fine as long as you make the initial stitches even," I say finally, and turn back to my comic.

Papers flew up into an arch over her head. With a little scream she fell backwards, arms wide.

We've been asked to tidy the exam-stock cupboard. She's standing on a chair and I'm handing stacks up to her.

The end-of-lunch bell rings, and footsteps come down the corridor. Lots of them, but I feel someone stop close behind me.

I glance over my shoulder, and see Eisuke. Hands in pockets, but hesitant. Good God, is he going to offer to help? Surely not, not before pigs take wing.

Makiko reaches up with her stack of papers. The stack's a considerable height now, and she's not. She strains.

As she and the papers cascade, a black shadow moves past me.

The next thing I see is Makiko safe in Eisuke's arms, looking up bewildered at him amid a sea of papers.

The silence of three seconds is an eternity, sometimes.

Without letting go of her, Eisuke reaches up and tears off his second button. Even in the surprise of the moment I notice it comes off very easily. Almost as if it's been loosened. He holds it out to her on an open palm.

Another eternity as she takes it, incredulous.

"Would you like some cookies?" she asks, finally.

I stumble backwards out towards class.

Things are not going to be the same.

Myths, Fables, and Legends

Ningyodashi
flash fiction by Fritz Bogott

My father climbed aboard our small boat and sailed out onto the land. My mother kept a vigil for two nights and a day, neither eating nor drinking. When his sails finally came back into view, she accepted a single cup of tea.

When my father was once again safely at sea, he stepped from the boat and apologized to my mother for his meager catch: Only a single scrawny calf had found its way into his nets. Together they butchered it and my mother hung its carcass below the waves.

They sent my brother (who though almost a man is deathly afraid of the land) a few yards up the beach to fetch the herbs that grow there. They taste and smell of earth--a smell that fills me with longing.

When the beef and the herbs were well-soaked, I sharpened my knife and cut translucent slices of each. These I brewed in boiling water until they had given up their flavor. I strained the broth and fed the exhausted dregs to the tiger shark who begs outside our door.

The broth? Such a simple thing. All at once it tastes of home and reminds us of the small dry world beyond.

Ice Maiden

flash fiction by JL Merrow

They said that I was cold, my sisters did, because I had no use for the young men of our village, with their harsh voices and their swaggering ways. They called me ice-maiden and snow-queen. They dragged me to the fire and pressed my face down close to its mocking red tongues, until my skin tightened and my breath withered in my throat, and I cried without making a sound.

"This will melt her heart!" one crowed.

"No, no; she has no heart, only a block of ice within her breast," another jeered. My father looked on, but did nothing to stop them, and I wept the harder as I saw that his frown was for me alone.

And so, when the moon had long since chased away the sun, and snowflakes fell thick as cherry blossom in the springtime winds, I ran from my village. I ran far; but when I looked back I saw my treacherous feet had left tracks upon the snow for all to follow. So I ran further still, into the forest, heedless of the many dangers that hide there: of Yuki-onna and Yama-uba, and the terrible *oni* with their fearsome tusks and iron clubs, who creep from the mountains to prey upon the unwary. My face and hands knew only pain, and my feet were like two blocks of wood affixed to the ends of my legs, but still I ran.

I ran until I came upon a clearing into which the moon shone brighter than the morning sun, and at once my discomforts were as nothing, for a dark-haired lady stood within the circle of the moon's light. In her arms was a tiny child. I gasped to see them; and then the child smiled at me and faded into smoke, leaving the lady standing alone.

She was more beautiful than the sunset; more beautiful than the first frosts of winter. Her kimono was white as the snow upon the mountaintops, and her skin like rice paper. Her lips were redder than cherries, and I wondered if it was true that she drank men's blood.

"Tell me your name, pretty child," she commanded me.

"I am Natsumi, my lady," I told her, my head bowed low.

"No, no! That will not do at all," she chided me, shaking her beauteous head slowly upon her slender neck, and I began to weep. "Pretty one, why do you cry?" she asked.

I wept harder, and hid my face with my hands. "You, who are so beautiful, you too think me cold, unworthy to bear the name of Summer Child."

"And for this you weep? Don't you know who I am?"

"I know who you are, my lady," I told her, as the wind froze my tears upon my cheeks. "You are Yuki-onna, who steals men's lives with a kiss."

"Yes," she told me, her tone regal. "I am Yuki-onna, maiden of snow; but what use have I for men with their hot passions and fiery tempers? It is a wicked slander, put about by those who would lie with me, and whom I refuse." She stepped forward, and traced one icy finger over my lips. "Those who call you cold are praising you, though they know it not. For the cold is a wonderful thing: it makes the land a place of beauty, and eases men's sufferings with a sigh. And it brings my children to me."

"Your children, my lady? I thought--but I must have been mistaken."

The lady smiled, and her teeth were like the ice upon the water-buckets in the first light of morning. "I have many children, my pretty one, and if you had come to me sooner you should have been one of them." She opened her arms, and I saw as if in a dream many dozens of small figures cluster around her. "They come to me at dusk, when their parents' eyes are weary. But you came to me by moonlight, so I shall call you Tsukiko, my moon-child, and you will come with me and be my love, and we shall be together always."

I wished so to go with her, but I was afraid. "My lady, what of my footprints? For my father's men will follow my tracks, and they will find you too."

"Then you must become as I am, dear Tsukiko, and they will never find us, save upon a winter's night far from shelter, when we may seek them out as the spirit takes us."

So I took her hand, and I left my two useless blocks of wood, and I ran with her and her laughing children.

And we left no mark of our passage save a flurry of snowflakes, and a whispered cold breath.

"Ice Maiden" was previously published in *The Archangel and the White Hart*, ed. by Jonathan Pinnock.

The Stonecutter
a poem by Martin Elster

Once upon a time there lived a stonecutter who went
each day to a whopping rock protruding from a mountain, sent
his hammer and his chisel to it, making slabs and blocks
for tombs and houses, understood the property of rocks,
was such a careful craftsman that he never lacked employment,
and for a time was quite content; the work gave him enjoyment.

Now, in the mountain dwelt a spirit. Sometimes it appeared
and aided men in growing rich and prosperous. Too weird
a notion for the workman, who had never seen this spirit.
A day was coming, though, when he would actually revere it.

One day he took a gravestone to the house of a wealthy fellow
and saw things never dreamed of. Then as if a dulcet cello
breathed music in his ears, he thought, "If only I were rich;
sleep in a silken-curtained bed. Hard work is such a bitch!

"Your wish is heard; you shall be rich," the mountain spirit spoke.
The stonecutter looked round. He thought it must have been a joke
his mind had played. He saw no one around. So then he strode
toward home with all his tools. But when he reached his small abode,
in place of his old wooden hut, there stood a palace, grand
as anything a man had ever seen in all the land.
Such splendid fittings, but the finest thing of all? The bed--
just like the one he'd envied! Now a new life lay ahead.

One dog-day morn the sun blazed so intensely, the stonecutter
stopped working. He could hardly breathe! All he could do was mutter
about how hot it was and went back home. That very night,
he peeped out through his blinds and saw a truly noble sight:
A little carriage drawn by servants dressed in silver and blue
passed by his house. A prince sat in the carriage. And the view
of a gold umbrella in his hand was just beyond belief!
Although the sight of all this lavishness was rather brief,
the fact the prince was shielded from the violent solar blaze,
produced a yearning in the man as burning as those rays:

"If I only were a prince." And then he was. His wide umbrella
was wonderful. But he was an eccentric sort of fella.
He looked around for something else to wish for. All his yard,
for all he watered it, was scorching. Not a thing could guard
his skin from burning. Even his umbrella couldn't do it.
The sun was hotter than a stove. How could the man subdue it?
The sun is mightier than his shade. "I wish I was the sun! "
The mountain spirit spoke: "Your wish is heard." And it was done.

He was the sun, and shot his beams and burnt the grass and fields,
and scorched the cheeks of princes, plus the penniless. The wheels
of might, however, started slowing in his heart and mind,
for there seemed nothing left to do to nature or mankind.
Dissatisfaction filled him. Then a cloud concealed his face.
Although he looked with fiery eyes at Earth, there was no trace
of it. He cried in anger, "Does a cloud confine my beams?
A cumulus is mightier than I? That's how seems.

If I only were a cloud!" And then he was. He lay between

the sun and Earth, which started growing riotous and green.

But then he started pouring rain, and rivers breached their bounds

and rice crops stood in water, and the villages and towns

were wrecked. Only the rock beside the mountain stood aloof.

The rock, immune to rain was, to the cloud, sufficient proof

that it was mightier than he. "If I only were the rock!"

And, once again, he caught the kindly mountain spirit's talk:

"Your wish is heard." The rock he was. Not rain nor heat could play

havoc with him now. "This is the best!" But then one day

he heard a puzzling noise around his feet, looked down, and spied

a big stonecutter driving chipping tools into his hide.

He shuddered from the shock. It split his ears. And then a great

and hefty block broke off and made the ground reverberate.

He cried, "Is a mere child of Earth mightier than a stone?

If I only were a man!" And then he was. Though every bone

and muscle in his body ached from labor and from toil

cutting stones again, he now was free from all turmoil.

He didn't want to be some other person or some thing.

His bed was hard, his food was scant yet, like a bird in spring,

he was content, and never asked for extra things again,

and didn't wish to be more powerful than other men.

At last he was a happy man, and never more would hear

the voice of the great mountain spirit rumbling in his ear.

"The Stonecutter" originally appeared in *Scarlet Literary Magazine*.

How the Fox Gained Entrance to Paradise

a story by Art Bupkis

There once was a monastery in the midst of an ancient forest. The monastery's large garden was more than the small community required, but foraging animals were a problem, so the monks built a high wall to keep them out.

Malaria beset the monks, too. The abbot in particular had frequent battles with its mind-clouding fevers. At such times he would leave the monastery to meditate at the forest's edge. There he would sit under the branches of a beautiful orchid-encrusted persimmon tree that spread for many meters over the wall from where it grew in the garden.

On this particular day the abbot's fever was more malignant than usual, and he collapsed before beginning his meditation. When he awakened, it was twilight, and there, close by, was an aged fox. The fox was leaping, time and time again, at a fine, ripe persimmon that hung a full four meters above its head. The abbot watched for many minutes, letting his mind clear before he addressed the animal.

"So foxes are not as clever as some would have us think. Will you continue all night?"

"There's nothing else I should do," the fox barked out as it continued leaping. Its concern was riveted on the fruit, not the priest.

Though obviously nearing exhaustion, with each leap at the persimmon the fox thrashed in the air like a great fish trying to clear a dam. As the spectacle continued the abbot felt himself becoming irritated, but did not know why. He decided to pursue the questions he could not suppress.

"Surely there is other food in this forest you can reach. Why do you persist in something that's clearly impossible?"

The fox paused to catch its breath before addressing the human.

"My obsession," it gasped. "I've been stricken by a desire to have the fruit of this one tree alone. Why? I do not know, but the tree is very beautiful, is it not? It may be that I cannot reach its fruit, but I simply will not resign myself to never having it."

"Do you try my intelligence?" the abbot wondered out loud. "Why don't you just dig under the wall, enter the garden, then climb the tree?"

"Easier said than done," the fox replied. "The garden, as you above all should remember, is patrolled by vicious dogs. I'd be torn to pieces the moment I set foot inside."

The abbot thought he was onto the fox's game, but could not be sure. Night had come and he wasn't able to discern the telltale expressions of the animal's face. He decided to be polite, but direct.

"I'm surprised a fox, such as yourself, hasn't tried conning some passer-by into knocking a persimmon down with a stick. Then you could cheat him out of it once it hit the ground."

"But the only one here is you!" cried the fox, suddenly agitated. "You're sick, and not up to the effort. Nor could I get it from you. You'd eat it yourself."

The abbot knew the fox spoke truly. His mood softened as it would toward a troubled novice.

"Maybe this fruit isn't worth the effort, even if you could get it. Despite its looks it might be over-ripe, fermented, and sour."

"I used to make such excuses in my youth," the fox replied wearily as it turned from the man to leap yet again.

The silver light of the full harvest moon streamed through the branches of the orchid-encrusted persimmon tree as fever flooded the priest's mind once again. Whether he was conscious, delirious--or merely dreaming--who can say? The grunts and thuds of the fox leaping, time and time again without success, continued for what seemed like hours.... or perhaps days.... or maybe only a moment. Who can say?

Nevertheless, when this time was up, the fox was dead.

Long after midnight the abbot arose and laid a fallen orchid on the corpse. He returned to the monastery by the soft light of the setting moon.

As he built a small pyre for the fox's remains the next day just outside the garden wall, the abbot thought of the "Six Persimmons" by the famous 13th c. Chan Buddhist painter, Mu Chi.

The abbot had been an artist, too, in his youth, and at that time had been consumed by an overwhelming desire to be the first of Mu Chi's admirers to re-embody the spirit of the original painting in a new rendition. He wasn't unusual. Conjuring the spirit of the "Six Persimmons" was, in fact, such a common dream among young artists of the day that the plight of one so afflicted had become something of a wistful joke.

When the passion of his obsession finally died of relentless failure, the abbot, like many before him, found success pursuing other things.

Still feverish, and exhausted from wood gathering under the midday sun, the abbot decided to nap in the shade while the fire burned itself out. Soon thin smoke spread through the forest like pale ink wash.

"Would you like a taste?" the fox whispered as it held a fine, ripe persimmon in front of the awakening man's lips.

"It was worth the effort, and now the fruit of the whole tree is mine!"

The delighted fox danced a gleeful jig, then leaped into the air. Spreading its translucent leather wings, it flew over the garden wall to the top of the orchid-encrusted persimmon tree.

"But how could this possibly be?" the abbot shook his head in drowsy disbelief.

"It's only karma," sang the flying fox as it glided back to earth. "Go ahead, take a bite. I want you to share this."

The confused abbot bit, and as he did, awakened some dreams once dead.

Kitsune by Shkna 9
(ink)

Silver Arrow

a story by Raven Dane

Hakata on Northern Kyushu, 1273

Matsu kept to the moonlight shadows. In the courtyard, warriors in full armour dismounted heavily from exhausted horses, the steam from the beasts' sweat-stained coats rising like the sea mist that rolled in from the bay. The girl knew she must not be seen; the thirteen-year-old daughter of a lowly peasant who helped care for the warhorses had no place among the haughty, noble samurai. Their mood was angry, their impatience dangerous. By their dour looks, the campaign to raise aid from neighbouring warlords against the foreign invaders had not gone well.

Matsu was frightened; she had listened as the older servants swapped horrific stories about raids from the sea against villages along the coast. The invaders came from a vast land, she heard, with plenty of room for all, so why did they want to attack the people of Japan? The only hope was men like these, valiant, honourable, steeped in the warrior code, of bushido…if they could not hold back the invaders, all would be lost.

She waited, looking for a familiar star-dappled white coat amongst the milling horses…Silver Arrow…her favourite. She endured such anguish whenever he was ridden out to battle. Like their riders, not all the horses returned from war and some came back injured, blood mixing with sweat on their muscular shoulders and flanks. Matsu's heart hammered, where was Silver Arrow? Then she saw him, behind a group of dark bays and chestnuts, his beautiful, distinctive coat now covered with mud and dried sweat, his head down between his knees with fatigue. Alarmed, she risked the wrath of the warriors and keeping tight to the walls surrounding the courtyard, made her way to the horse.

It was soon apparent, the samurai had only one thought…to rest, be ready to ride again at the next sign of trouble. They did not notice the slender girl pick up the reins of the grey horse and lead it to shelter. Alone with the horse, Matsu tucked up the hem of her plain woven kimono and did her best to make Silver Arrow comfortable. She remembered what to do from watching her father, keeping Silver Arrow away from too much cold water, allowing him a few sips until he had fully recovered. She eased off the tight girth, the buckles slippery with hot, salty sweat, hauling off the heavy saddle and wool blanket. The unexpected sheer weight made her lose her balance and fall onto the straw with a loud gasp of surprise. For a few moments, she lay winded and bruised, pinned down by the lacquered wood and leather saddle.

Another horse may well have spooked by the child's awkward fall beneath its feet, possibly trampling her with its iron-shod hooves but Silver Arrow stood quietly. He turned his head to look at her with his dark eyes. Determined not to be a useless girl like the pampered daughters of the warlord, Matsu shoved the saddle aside and scrambled back onto her feet. She grabbed a big handful of clean straw and began to wipe the mud and sweat from Silver Arrow's coat. The steady, rhythmic brushing felt good to the horse, he relaxed his long neck and gave a deep sigh. At one point, he nuzzled Matsu's face with his grey velvet nose, blowing softly in greeting.

Committed to doing her best, Matsu worked for hours, only stopping when the horse's coat shone like the silver shimmer of a ghost koi on a sunlight-dappled pond. He had recovered enough to eat the hay she brought him, wisps of which stuck in her hair and clothes. His contented munching lulled her to a deep slumber, nestled in the thick, dry bedding.

She awoke, startled by a harsh cough of displeasure. Matsu scrambled to her feet in alarm and dropped onto her knees, bowing her head to touch the ground at the feet of the Daimyo, the high-ranking warlord himself.

"What is this intrusion? How dare you disturb the rest of my horse! "

Matsu quivered with fear, knowing the swish of his sword scything through the air would be the last she'd ever hear.

"My lord, I meant no harm. Silver Arrow was exhausted, covered with thick mud. I made him comfortable, that is all."

"You will turn him into a placid pet like an old brood mare," the Daimyo snarled, "a warhorse should be aloof, suspicious, fierce."

Matsu found a hidden well of courage within her, if she was going to die by the warlord's sword, she might as well express her opinion freely,

"It is not the way of the warrior to temper ferocity with benevolence? A kind heart is no less courageous in the height of battle?"

The Daimyo, Takamori bent down and raised up her chin, studying her face with a curious expression, before bidding her to stand up. How strange for this daughter of a lowly servant to know one of the tenants of bushido. To have the courage to respect yet not fear him.

"You did this all by yourself? Made Silver Arrow's coat shine like silk?" Takamori questioned her, stroking the curve of the horse's muscular neck, the threat no longer in his manner. Matsu nodded with pride.

"And can you ride?"

The girl hesitated to answer, she had taught herself, late at night out in the fields, riding the brood mares without saddle or bridle. Learning to control the quiet mothers by shifting her weight and balance and by voice. Something any servant, let alone a chit of a girl was forbidden to do.

Takamori could see her fear and tried to reassure her, "Child if you can ride, I will spare you any punishment."

Hesitant, dreading a cruel ruse, Matsu nodded, surprised at the sigh of relief on the young warlord's stern face.

"Then we have been granted a sign of hope…for you must share the spirit and blood of Tomoe Gozen…the legendary *onna bugeisha*."

It was Matsu's turn to be astonished…everyone knew the stories about the famous female samurai warrior. Once a concubine to Emperor Minamoto no Yoshinaka, she excelled in swordsmanship and use of the *naginata* and rode the wildest horses with ease. She won great honour in many battles including the Genpei War. She died in peace from old age, treated with honour and respect by all.

That was the last night Matsu spent under her father's roof. The warlord took her into his own household as his ward. To the astonishment of the entire Takamori retinue, he demanded that the girl was schooled in the art of bushido alongside the boys of her age. Ignoring their scorn, she learnt to ride swift, powerful warhorses using saddles and bridles, to wield the deadly *naginata*—a long lance tipped with a sharp blade, to be agile, fearless and proud. Yet she was still able to enjoy stolen many moments with her family, her life had found a strange, thrilling direction yet with a pleasing balance.

Not so the atmosphere prevailing across the land. As the weeks rolled on, the number of attacks from the sea dwindled to nothing. Expectation of invasion turned to nervous anticipation then to dangerous complacency. Only the coastal-based Daimyo kept up their vigilance, their training of troops, warning beacons kept dry.

Matsu had grown taller and stronger yet without sacrificing her femininity and natural willowy grace. With the prospect of war fading, she often wondered what her future would be now. Her role as the embodiment of the valiant spirit of Tomoe Gozen had no purpose in a peaceful Japan. Even the murderous, ever simmering blood feuds between the noble houses had ceased.

The days of normal life returning across the lands were to be short-lived. In the summer of 1274, her sleeping form silvered by a full moon filtering into her chamber, the night erupted into mayhem as the household awoke in alarm. Mariners from a small fleet of fishing boats had beached their craft in their panic to spread a warning. Horsemen from the coastal villages spread the word inland. An invading fleet of great magnitude approached Japan's western shores. At first Daimyo and warriors alike were sceptical. The size of the invading armada must be exaggerated, fisherman's tall tales like the size of fish that had got away from their nets. Such talk of over 600 ships, laden with warriors, horses, catapults and flaming rockets was impossible.

Wisdom overcame incredulity. Takamori cast aside all doubts, the fishing fleet had risked wrecking their precious craft and with them their livelihoods in their haste to sound the alarm. Not something done on the strength of exaggeration. He summoned his cavalry and sent messengers out to gather all men capable of wielding a weapon. Any weapon be it only a humble rice flail. He brought Matsui a set of gleaming red and gold trimmed armour in person, bowing his head as he presented it to her.

"Ride at the head of my army on Silver Arrow, Matsu…fan the spark of hope to a blazing inferno of victory."

Overcome, the girl dropped to the floor both in respect to the warlord and to hide her fear. Sparring with the lads in mock battles was all she had known, but now she faced the reality of the blood, terror and pain of battle. How could she, the daughter of a stable hand become valiant and fierce as a samurai? She was just Matsui…not Tomoe Gozen!

Within the hour, all the mounted warriors pushed their excited horses swiftly down the coastal road; from all directions men on foot joined the following army. Matsu's hands shook too much to control Silver Arrow by the reins, too nervous to do anything but keep her balance in the high, padded saddle. The horse knew his duty, refusing to jink or spook at shadows or men suddenly breaking through the night, waving swords and crying out in a show of bravado. He trotted along calmly, surefooted and brave, his silver ears pricked forward. Gradually the horse's steady demeanour spread to his rider…normally it was the rider whose mood affected the horse. Focusing on her duty, Matsu was determined not to fail and she was calm by the time Takamori's army reached a high point overlooking a stretch of beach, the sea calm, the wind set fair in the invader's favour.

The Daimyo turned to address Matsu, his voice low so as not to spread alarm.

"Child, today, we may face a force of over twenty--thousand troops, determined men from the enemy nations. They will bring a new form of warfare to our lands, machines that throw big rocks over great distances, things that fly screaming like demons above our heads and rain down fire on our people. We train from childhood to fight with honour, man to man. We will have no defence against this slaughter."

The warlord gripped his sword and sighed, "But we have no choice, we cannot turn away from out duty to defend our lands. Ride, Matsu, ride down past the ranks, fill the men with the heroic spirit of Tomoe Gozen. There is nothing left but our courage."

As instructed, Matsu cantered along the ranks of men on foot and cavalry, a banner in the Takamori colours attached to the back of the saddle and proudly streaming behind her. The sight of the slender female samurai so at ease on the powerful, beautiful silver horse worked its magic, her call for pride and bravery answered with a resounding cheer that passed through the ranks to rise above them like a banner of defiance to the nearing enemy.

She returned to the Daimyo, relieved to see the look of satisfaction gleam on his severe face. She had lived up to his hopes and fulfilled her destiny to be the spirit of Tomoe Gozen. In silence, Matsu positioned the horse behind the warlord and waited for the invaders to reach their shores. As the first dark shapes breached the horizon, it was clear the fishermen had not exaggerated. Soon the distant meeting place of sea and sky was a sold line of dark sails. So many! Yet again, the warlord sent Matsui to ride along the ranks, urging courage and determination…this time he rode at her side to reinforce his belief in her message.

As she finally halted Silver Arrow, she knew something was wrong. Very wrong. The normally well-mannered horse became increasingly agitated, pulling free from the reins and head high, he began to glance to the east, snorting with unease. As she struggled to control him, the anxiety gradually began to spread to the other horses. The Daimyo glared in fury at Matsu, blaming her lack of experience for allowing her horse to upset the others at such a crucial time for raised moral and self-control.

Before she could admonish and rein in the fractious beast, the first forerunner of a windstorm created dust devils in the sand below them. The branches of nearby trees began to stir in a stiff breeze that smelt of rain. Another dark line appeared on the horizon, broader, faster and higher. Within minutes, the offshore breeze became strong, lashing at the waiting army with debris and stinging sand. Silver Arrow now was a whirl of agitated, trampling anxiety, whinnying and trying to turn towards home.

"My lord," Matsu called above the screeching wind, "this must be warning of a typhoon heading our way...the horse is right...we must go inland to save your army. There is no time to lose."

The girl was right...Takamori knew well the early signs of a deadly storm and these warnings spoke of a monstrous typhoon on its way. But what of loss of face? Of honour?

Seeing his hesitation, Matsu gambled with her life...what was one girl compared to that of so many brave men? The beloved sons, brothers and husbands of so many families. Driving her heels into Silver Dollars flanks, she spurred on, pushing the horse out of an alarmed high rear.

"Return to your homes and make your families safe from the coming storm." Matsu shouted to the army, "The Kamikaze....the divine wind is on its way to protect us from the invaders. Return swiftly with honour to your homes."

There was no hesitation, all of a certain age recognised the signs of a coming typhoon. One that would shatter and scatter the enemy fleet like wooden toys crushed under a heavy booted heel. Nothing could withstand its force, not even the highest ambitions of greedy foreign rulers.

By now, the roiling black band of lightning straked cloud had swallowed the horizon, an unnatural darkness shrouded the land and heavy rain laced with ice shards carried on the wind towards the shore. Already, the tempest had obscured all sight of the invading fleet. With his own horse plunging frantically, eager for flight, Takamori knew the girl was right. The great wind would destroy the evil threatening his homeland but it would also endanger its defenders. They must head inland and let the typhoon protect them.

Matsu gave a low groan of relief as the warlord signalled retreat. With Silver Arrow's head turned towards inland and home, the great beast leaped forward and took off in an instinctive bolt, there was nothing Matsu could do to control him. With the wind-driven rain now straking at her face like demonic talons, she leant low over his withers and neck, burying her face into the thick strands of wet mane, relying on his eyesight and homing skills to get her back to safety.

Within minutes, the storm sent branches and roof tiles from distant villages whirling like weapons but Silver Arrow ran on, dodging or jumping any peril thrown in his way. Matsu saw nothing of this, unable to do anything but cling onto the horse's neck and keep flattened low, her feet jammed hard into the stirrups for more balance as Silver Arrow jinked and swerved mid head long gallop. All measure of time had tuned into the steady drumming of galloping hooves and pounding heartbeats.

Sodden, wind battered and exhausted, Matsu was somehow aware the sound of the wind was now deadened by surrounding walls, of her horse halting , his sides heaving, valiant heart hammering. Of strong hands gently lifting her from the saddle. Then gentler, sweet scented hands removing her armour and garb, enveloping her in warm, dry wool. Then sleep.

Matsu awoke to a world scoured by the storm. Many homes had fallen but would be rebuilt. Many trees felled but others would grow in their place. Sad losses softened by the joy of future newborns. She went to see the silver horse and found him resting, contently munching his hay. Tears of gratitude traced a route down her face as she put her arms around his broad neck. This noble beast had saved her life... maybe many more with his early warning of the approaching typhoon. She had already learnt that the enemy fleet had been destroyed...the loss so great, the invaders would need many years to assemble another.

Her homeland was at times transcendently beautiful, as gentle as the cherry blossom in spring or the first fall of winter snow. But many times the earth beneath them would heave and shake or great winds and waves batter its shores. Such adversity had tempered its people, given them resilience, courage and resolution to re-build and carry on. Given them the knowledge that life was too fleeting, too precious not to cherish and continue on living.

Matsu looked deep into the gentle, dark brown eyes of the horse and he stopped eating and returned her gaze with the curious, quizzical nature of his kind. Two such different beings, joined in mutual affection, gentle nature and yet when challenged, unshakable courage born of loyalty and duty. In future, if needed, she would wear the mantle of Tomoe Gozen with honour and pride.

Footnote: The enemy leader realized that nature, not military incompetence, had been the cause of his forces' failure in 1274 so, in 1281, he launched a second invasion. Seven weeks of fighting took place in north western Kyushu before another typhoon struck, again destroying his fleet.

Moon Kisses

a story by Heidi Mannan

Moonlight winked off Tokiko's glossy black hair, which fell across her shoulders like silk worth an entire year's wages.

Rai couldn't help but stare. "Are we getting close?" He dipped an oar into the icy water, forcing his eyes from the girl and watching beads of liquid light fall when he lifted the oar out again.

"I think we need to veer right," Tokiko said.

Rai looked up at her. "That's Tanaka Tanuma's land."

"He doesn't live there." Her voice crept across the night from a face as white as the recent snowfall.

"Did you know that land is cursed?" Rai asked.

"It's not."

"That's why Tanaka Tanuma doesn't live there anymore."

Her tiny mouth curved downward as she tilted her head. "I've been there many times."

He stared at her, finding omens in her every breath and blink. The air dodged his lungs for a few attempted breaths. "You scare me."

Her eyes, nothing but black voids, leveled on him, freezing his blood.

"All I know about you is your name," Rai said. "Where're you from?"

"I don't know you well enough to tell you."

"Well, I don't know you, either. If you refuse to tell me about yourself, you'll remain an enigma."

"Does it matter?"

"At least tell me why it's so important you get to Tanaka Tanuma's land tonight."

"I told you I'd pay you in peaches as soon as we get back. I stay true to my word."

Rai heard water lapping the shore. They were getting close. When his boat hit solid ground, the raw-earth scent of lake mud wafted into the air. A forest set in deep shadow spread before them, thin mist weaving around tree trunks.

"So what?" Rai asked, looking around. "What's so spectacular about this place?"

"We aren't there yet." Tokiko climbed from the boat as though she'd indeed done this before. "What?" she asked when Rai didn't follow. "You really afraid of some silly curse?"

"No." But his body wouldn't move out of the boat.

"I'm going," Tokiko said. "Come if you want." After only a few footsteps, shadows swallowed her.

"Wait," Rai said, not certain she could even hear him in all that darkness. "I can't let you go alone."

Her laugh sounded more mature than her age, floating from among the trees. Rai wasn't sure it was her, but followed the sound anyway.

"I don't need a man to keep me safe." It was Tokiko's voice. "Especially one who's afraid of everything."

He tailed her dark silhouette over fallen branches that snapped beneath their feet, the moon peeking at them from between the trees every now and then. The snow hadn't touched the earth here, the canopy of evergreens too dense.

The forest eventually opened into a small, snow-covered clearing. Tokiko stepped into the open space and stopped. Moonlight instantly tangled with her hair. She pointed to the left. "Tanaka Tanuma's old tea house is that way. This is his garden."

Upon close inspection, Rai recognized a few dormant ornamentals half hidden by weeds and snow, trying to push toward heaven.

"Why do you come here?" he asked.

She pointed across the clearing. In the white light of the moon, a giant flowering plum stood like a king, his crown a multitude of glowing red petals.

Tokiko drew closer to the king, obviously his most loyal subject.

Rai followed, mesmerized by what looked like blood dotting the branches, all those petals, vibrant even in the moonlight.

"We got here just in time," Tokiko said.

"In time for…"

Tokiko placed her fingers over his lips as she stared at the tree.

He followed her gaze. As his vision again met the tree, petals rained to earth, falling over them, brushing across his cheeks like thousands of tiny moon kisses. He tasted the cold air in his mouth as his jaw hung, his arms limp at his sides. Every other sensation left his mind, his body. Every worry, large and small, melted and floated away on the petals, falling onto snow, red against white. They were the only things left in the world, those magnificent blossoms.

A delicate carpet lay at their feet. Tokiko waited until the very last petal seesawed to the earth, and then her voice crept across the night. "It happens every year. If it's a curse, I must be a demon, because no matter what else happens during the year, this moment brings me endless pleasure."

Where he earlier saw omens in Tokiko's pale face, Rai now saw a deity. He saw beauty unmatched by any human, beauty more like the red petals falling through moonlight.

They spoke not a word on the return journey. As soon as Rai docked the boat, Tokiko jumped out. "Wait here and I'll bring the peaches."

"Don't bother."

"I told you I'd give them to you. I'm not a cheat."

"I changed my mind. I don't want peaches. I want something else."

Her black pearl eyes stared at him.

"Promise you'll meet me here next year," he said. "Same time."

Her small mouth broadened. "See you next year." And she vanished into the night.

Satori vs. Non-Satori

flash fiction by Lisa Scullard

As the cherry blossom was starting to fall, samurai retainers Doko and Kyuma decided to settle their differences. Doko was of the *satori* school of thought, to whom experience, training, preparation, research and practise were the key to success; while Kyuma, who believed only in luck and Fate, was non-*satori*.

They had argued many days and nights over whose faith was correct, and each hoped the other would suffer a defeat in battle to prove their argument. But both still lived, and the continued dispute became a petty, tiresome issue to all those burdened to listen to their reports on the debate.

"My Lord's wife yawns whenever I am in sight," Doko thought, torturing his mind only further at the injustice. "I will seek to prove that *satori* is the only way to win."

"My luck has held, but I should like to test it further," Kyuma pondered. "The arrogance of the *satori* that they control their own destiny, and the Fate of others through dedication to rehearsal and preparation, is becoming a cult of the ego and an insult to the gods."

So, it was as the flowers shed their first petals, that the two samurai met by the lake.

"I have executed a dozen prisoners this morning," announced Doko. "Just so that my striking blade shall not feel the resistance of your neck."

"I am not a prisoner," Kyuma replied simply. "I am here with just my free will and a fresh sword."

"I rehearsed two dozen killing cuts, one hundred times apiece," Doko continued.

"I slept well," Kyuma nodded. "And I had pleasant dreams."

"I have written my words for your funeral," Doko countered.

"I drank a toast to our meeting," Kyuma said. "There is a drop left, if you wish to share."

The delicate petals swirled around them, shearing into pieces where they touched the patiently awaiting blades.

"The gods await the outcome of our experiment," said Doko. "My Lord awaits justice."

"The gods certainly await one of us," Kyuma agreed.

Out of the swirling petals, a lone butterfly appeared and landed on the tip of his finger. Its tongue uncurled, tasting the surface.

"Look at the creature," Doko scorned. "It thinks you are a flower. It must be time for your blossom to fall."

"Or maybe it is time for my pollen to spread," Kyuma suggested. "Let us wait for it to finish."

The butterfly flexed its wings and flew directly to Doko's breast. Tasting again.

"The creature is confused," Doko grumbled. "Most likely it has been at your *sake* also."

"It is looking for your heart, I think," Kyuma suggested.

It seemed a long time passed before the butterfly stretched again, and fluttered away on the breeze.

"I am very tired," said Doko, at last. "I do not feel I could do this challenge justice after such a long day, and not enough training beforehand."

"Sleeping well is part of good preparation," Kyuma agreed. "I, myself, am a little drunk. Perhaps I am forgetting why we are here."

"I need to practise more," Doko nodded. "Tomorrow, I will be fully prepared. I will rehearse two hundred times beforehand."

"I will chance my luck at gambling, or perhaps a new mistress," Kyuma mused. "If I survive, maybe luck will shine on me tomorrow, too."

At certain times of year, beside a certain lake—if you look carefully, you will see two indentations in the grass where the petals never fall. For Doko and Kyuma still return in spirit, one dedicated to honing his skills before the final duel; the other at chancing his luck first in every possible manner...

108

Old and New

The Unfortunate Incident of the Broken Weenie
a story by Damien C. Edwards

Satoko Inoue was sipping tea when she heard a thunk. The sound, while quite ordinary in itself, was unusual and quite unexpected in her house. She looked around and saw Jun standing in the entrance to the room, immobile and if possible, slightly startled.

"Jun?"

He looked up at her, "Madam, I seem to have…"

She waited but when he didn't continue, she felt a small stab of anxiety twitter along the lining of her stomach. "Jun, is there something wrong?"

"Yes madam, I appear to have…" he looked down at his feet, hesitating before he said without any humour, "I appear to have dropped my penis."

Satoko covered her mouth to stifle a gasp and made her way over to him. "How did it…?"

"I don't know madam, one moment I was coming in to join you and the next it…it just fell off."

"Oh dear," she looked around his feet, "Where is it now?"

"I think it's somewhere in the vicinity of my left ankle, madam, under the leg of my pants."

She bent down to gain a better vantage but stopped herself before she touched him. She looked up, "May I?"

It was only for a fraction of a second but she noticed the hesitation before he replied, "Of course, madam."

She reached out and lifted his trouser leg. The head was resting on the ground against his foot and when she prodded, the rest flopped onto the *tatami* mat with a flap. She picked it up and examined the base. There were a number of detached wires, a couple of pistons, possibly broken, and what looked to her like plumbing. She looked up at his wide unblinking eyes and said, "Jun, I'm so sorry."

"Yes madam," he said and again she noted an edge of discomfort.

"Don't you worry about this though," she said, hoping she sounded more confident than she felt, "We're going to get this fixed and if we can't, we'll get you a new one."

But she wasn't so sure, Jun was an old model, she kept him around for what she told herself was nostalgia, because he was her first, but if she was to be honest with herself, she kept him because her affection for him was closer to that of love, rather than an attachment to a possession. She hadn't made love to Jun in many years, she had more recent models for that, models with finer dexterity and modern software more suitable for someone of her age, but he was her constant companion and she knew she wouldn't feel altogether right if he wasn't complete. And, she thought, it appears that he wouldn't either.

Satoko called for her maid. The maid was a modern model and much to Satoko's displeasure, they never made them plain or ugly by default, always a constant reminder of her own lost youth, so as a petty and somewhat pointless act of meanness, Satoko had never given the maid a name, only ever referring to her by her function.

"Madam?" the maid said, coming up behind Jun.

"Connect me to AAV Systems."

The maid blinked once and said in a voice that wasn't her usual operating voice, "Welcome to AAV Systems, how can we assist your inquiry?"

Satoko briefly wondered if there was a tactful way to explain the situation but decided on the direct approach, "My android's penis has fallen off."

"Is this problem regarding the model you are currently calling from?"

"No, wait, what? The maid comes with a penis?"

"Not in the standard model but it is a popular customisation."

Satoko looked speculatively at the maid, then shaking her head she said, "It's an Alpha four."

"One moment while I connect you to a special representative."

The maid stood blankly for few seconds of silence before a man's voice spoke through her, "Good morning Ms Inoue," Satoko always found a human voice relayed through an android disturbing because there wasn't a direct interface, resulting in a fractional delay to the movement of the lips. "My name is Hashimoto, special representative. You said there is a problem with your Alpha four."

"Yes, his penis has fallen off... Can you fix him?"

"Uh, I'm sorry to say but probably not. It has been many years since compatible parts were manufactured and even if we were able to find replacements, anyone who would have been able to do the repairs has long since retired. I'm sorry. From what I can tell here, you may have the only functional model in almost original condition."

"If I remember correctly," Satoko thoughtfully turned the cock in her hands, "He came with a lifetime warranty, well, I'm still alive."

"Indeed... What I can do for you is replace his body with one of our newer models, we can do a memory dump so there shouldn't be any difference to the personality."

"Will he look the same?"

"Cosmetically yes, however, the hardware will be far superior and be able to better withstand... rigorous activities."

"How old do you think I am?" She smiled in spite of herself.

"I'm sorry madam, that isn't what I meant, well it is, but not in the way it was understood. You see, the Alpha four was originally designed as a Lovedroid and early models had fairly unsophisticated base programming, namely to fulfill one particular task. If that base task is no longer required of them in the normal course of events, they may seek alternative avenues to fulfill that programming. For the Alpha four, a broken, uh, detached penis is not an uncommon consequence of android to android coupling."

Satoko saw what appeared to be guilt flash across Jun's face and felt a rush of anger and jealousy at the maid standing there with her apparent youth and detached beauty.

"I see," she said, "I think I may have to get back to you about any possible upgrades."

"Okay, I'll…"

"Disconnect." She shook the cock at the maid, "I think I've thought of a suitable name for you after all."

Godzilla's tea

flash fiction by David Church Rodríguez

As I sit down, he fumbles with the teapot and drops it. His hands are just too big. He starts apologizing and I can tell he feels really bad about it, as if he has somehow insulted me, so I walk up to his leg and give him a big hug.

"Don't worry," I say. "You're still my favourite monster."

Cherry Blossom Reverie
a poem by Martin Elster

(On Hearing Keiko Abe Play the Marimba)

As mallets frolic, leap and fall
and blur into a cloud of flowers,
the rosewood fills the spacious hall

with dazzling white sakura showers
borne from the tree we picnicked under,
all our minutes, all our hours

passing like this tuneful wonder
quickening my memory
and, wild as taiko-drumming-thunder,

we danced beneath that floral tree
that shook the garlands from its hair.
That night I dreamed a glorious sea

of petals washed ashore, the air,
the land, our very souls in thrall
to blossoms blowing everywhere.

I see you whirling in the squall,
as mallets frolic, leap and fall.

Footnote: Keiko Abe is a Japanese composer and marimba player, whose composition entitled "Dream of the Cherry Blossoms" is a standard of the marimba repertoire.

"Cherry Blossom Reverie" originally appeared in *Victorian Violet Press*.

Shogun Dreams
a story by Robert J. McCarter

Jeffery Smith was a wholly unremarkable man. He was neither old, nor young; neither short, nor tall; neither skinny, nor fat, although he did have the appropriate middle-aged bulge around his waist. He dressed unremarkably in jeans, which he looked slightly awkward in, and a long sleeved white dress shirt buttoned all the way up to the top. Even his phobias were entirely unremarkable: spiders, airplanes, and intimacy.

He was the kind of man that would go to a party and no one would remember he had been there. When Jeffery left a job it often took his coworkers several days (or even weeks) to realize that he was gone.

He was dying, but in the most common way. Stage 4 non-small cell lung cancer had just been discovered. Statistically speaking—and being an accountant, Jeffery knew statistics—he didn't have much time.

But today, on this Monday in March, Jeffery felt remarkable. The previous week he had gone in to see his doctor for a cough that would not go away. He was surprised by the call from the office to come in (he thought he had the flu, or maybe even bronchitis). He was even more surprised when his doctor solemnly told him of his diagnosis. There would be MRIs and more tests to type the cancer and determine the treatment, but the doctor was sure of the diagnosis.

And, perhaps most surprising, is what Jeffery did after the appointment: he went to his place of employment, the accounting offices of Richards, Parson, Thomas, and Gosling, and promptly gave his two weeks' notice. When he told his boss, Alan Gosling, the news, Mr. Gosling promptly sent him on to HR, and HR seeing that he had nearly 100 days of vacation and sick leave accrued told him to pack up his cubicle and leave. Now.

And so he did, filling a banker box with his few meager possessions: a tiny flag of Japan, some anime action figures, a few manga, a Final Fantasy IV poster, and other miscellaneous office flotsam.

Jeffery was dazed by the suddenness of it all, although he was not surprised; he knew he was just a salaryman, an easily replaceable cog in the workings of Richards, Parson, Thomas, and Gosling. He stood outside, banker box in hand, for a full five minutes wondering what to do. Then something remarkable occurred to him, so he walked to the bus stop and took the bus to the mall.

With the banker box in hand, Jeffery Smith stood at the front counter of Dream Makers. He had stood there for some three minutes, but the receptionist hadn't noticed him. This was normal. He studied her, as he often did when people didn't notice him. She was young and thin and beautiful with blond hair, very white teeth, and was showing a slightly more than tasteful amount of cleavage. Unremarkably, he did not mind waiting.

When she finally looked up and noticed him standing there, she said, "Welcome to Dream Makers. How can we make your dreams come true?"

"Umm…" he began. "Ahh…" he continued. Jessica (which is what it said on the receptionist's name tag), just sat there smiling evenly, showing off her dazzling smile and perfect teeth. "Well… You see…" Jeffery continued to stammer and start. "I want to dream."

"Excellent," Jessica said. "Just one moment and I will have one of our Dream Specialists come speak with you."

*

Jeffery Smith sat across from Dream Specialist Mindy Miner. She too was beautiful, with a dazzling white smile, and plentiful cleavage on display. But, she was a brunette, not a blond. Something for everyone, Jeffery thought.

"Would you like some coffee?" she asked.

Jeffery paused, normally he only had the one cup in the morning, but today was different, today was special. "Yes please."

"How do you take it?"

"One sugar with cream."

When Jessica had delivered the coffee Mindy smiled at him and said, "What dream can we fulfill for you today, Mr. Smith?"

Suddenly over being shy about his dream Jeffery let it come tumbling out. "Japan! I want to experience an epic adventure in the land of the rising sun. It should take place in the 17th century and start off like the mini-series Shogun, but end happily with the daring English adventurer finding love and embracing the new culture as his own."

Jeffery had watched Shogun with his father when he was eight years old (over the strenuous objections of his mother). It was then that he had fallen in love with the Japanese culture. Much of his adult leisure activities revolved around Japan: manga, anime, aikido, faulting attempts to learn the language, and tending to his three bonsai trees.

"Very good, Mr. Smith. We can do that. I presume you have seen the mini-series numerous times?"

"Oh yes, at least twice a year since the DVD came out."

"Very good, that will help. And I suppose you would like our deluxe package, which includes: extended REM; advanced hypnosis—"

"Yes, yes, all of that. It will feel real, right?"

"Absolutely real. Guaranteed."

The interview went on for quite some time with Mindy asking specific, and often embarrassing, questions about what he wanted to experience. Nudity? Sex? How much sex? How explicit should the sex be? Even what positions he liked and attributes of his preferred sexual partner. He answered these questions, slowly, with his face beet red and came to the conclusion that the typical Dream Makers client wanted to dream of sex and romance.

*

On Tuesday Jeffery Smith went to see the Dream Makers physician, Doctor Chahel Sen for a physical. Doctor Sen was a beautiful man with shiny black hair, smooth brown skin, and kind brown eyes. Jeffery was worried that his health condition would cause problems. When he told Doctor Sen of his diagnosis the doctor asked, "Are you currently being treated?"

"No," Jeffery answered. "Not yet. They still have more tests to do before a treatment plan can be determined."

"Then it will not be a problem sir. Many of our clients come to us as after a diagnosis such as yours."

Jeffery felt sad to hear this. He thought for once in his life he was doing something remarkable. It was upsetting to hear his reaction was common.

On Wednesday he went to the Dream Makers psychologist, Doctor Karen Thompson. She too was beautiful, with long brown hair and shining blue eyes. But, much to Jeffery's relief, she was not displaying any cleavage.

They started with a brief hypnosis test (to make sure he was a good candidate) that left Jeffery with a brief and shining image of him fighting Darth Vader with a samurai sword. Maybe it was her affable manner, maybe she had done something while he was hypnotized, but soon she had him talking with ease about his parents, his childhood, and how he felt about his diagnosis.

As he was leaving she asked him one last question, "Why don't you just go to Japan, Jeffery?"

"What?" he asked, surprised by the question. He couldn't imagine that particular question was Dream Makers approved.

"You long to see Japan; you could just get on a plane and go see it."

"Well…I…You see…" he stammered. "I don't have much time. I want the epic adventure." He didn't mention, what was perhaps, the real reason: his fear of airplanes.

On Friday he received a call from Dream Makers telling him that he had passed his exams with flying colors and that development of his program was well under way. Was he available for a Monday evening appointment?

The rest of Friday and the weekend passed with excruciating slowness. He spent his time watching Shogun, Godzilla movies, Memoirs of a Geisha, Cowboy Beebop, Ghost in the Shell, and many other of his favorite Japanese movies. Interspersed with his movie watching, he went to the dojo twice to practice aikido (or "falling down and getting up" as Sensei referred to it), ordered and ate Japanese takeout, and danced around the room singing: "Turning Japanese, I think I'm turning Japanese, I really think so".

*

On Monday at 6 pm sharp, a limo arrived at Jeffery Smith's apartment and took him to the Dream Makers sleep facility. There he was greeted by Doctor Alan Michaels. The doctor wore glasses, a white coat, and was rather unremarkable looking—he found this very comforting.

Jeffery was seated in a small room with a bed, two chairs, and some medical equipment. "How does it work?" He asked.

"Our approach is three pronged," Doctor Michaels began. "First we use a mild psychotropic that will make you more open to suggestion and make your dreams significantly more vivid. Second we use a proprietary drug that will deepen and lengthen your REM sleep and enhance your recollection of your dreams. And, thirdly we use hypnosis before and during your dream to create the experience you want."

"What if something goes wrong?"

Doctor Michaels smiled, "We monitor you the whole time. Relax, Jeffery; I've done this thousands of times. You are going to love your shogun experience."

*

Jeffery Smith sat across from Mindy Miner for his post-dream interview. He felt like a new man. He hadn't shaved in several days, and the top button on his long sleeved white dress shirt was left undone.

"Samurai swords, epic battles, beautiful women. It was…It was amazing." He paused, his brow furrowing. "I am still having dreams; really, really vivid dreams."

Mindy smiled, typing on her keyboard. "That is what we like to hear."

"But…" Jeffery began, before a coughing fit overtook him.

"Is it your health issue?" Mindy asked.

"Maybe, I don't know. I think I may be having some re-entry difficulties. I finally did something remarkable and now my life is just not interesting anymore. I mean…I quit my job and blew a ton of money on this. What am I going to do now? Wait to die?"

Mindy nodded and frowned. "You know what? Your plan comes with a follow-up visit with Doctor Thompson. Why don't you go see her? Here's her card."

As he got up to leave, Mindy said, "Oh. One more thing, Mr. Smith." She handed him what looked like a mini samurai sword about 6 inches long. "Open the flap on the end of the pommel; it's a USB drive with copies of the images we used in your hypnosis. You may find them useful in remembering, and reinforcing, your dream."

Jeffery left in a daze and went to the dojo to practice. Even that had paled; he was limited by his own skill, his own ability, unlike in his shogun dreams.

Jeffery Smith didn't go to see Doctor Thompson until a week later. By that time his shogun dreams of Japan had faded and he had fallen into a deep depression. Lung cancer; pending radiation treatments; parents dead; no relationship—where was the adventure? What was he going to do?

At first, he had decided not to go see her, but then he remembered what she had asked: Why don't you just go to Japan, Jeffery?

It stuck in his head. Why didn't he? Well, he was deathly afraid of flying, there was that. What if he wasn't? What if he could fly? He had enough money in savings to go, what else was his money good for now? What if he could get treatments in Japan? What if he could study aikido in Japan? What if he could study Japanese in Japan?

These thoughts swirled around his head during a long, sleepless night. In the morning he called Doctor Thompson's office and found there was cancelation for that very afternoon.

Jeffery Smith did not look his normal self. He was dressed in sweats and a t-shirt, his hair was messy, his face unshaven, and he had dark circles under his eyes. He sat slouched in a chair across from Doctor Karen Thompson.

"What is on your mind, Jeffery?" she asked.

"I want to go to Japan," he replied.

She nodded and smiled. "Good, I think that is a good step."

"But…" Jeffery began before going silent.

After a lengthy pause Doctor Thompson prompted, "But what?"

Jeffery shook his head. "Ohhh. There are so many buts. But, I am afraid of flying. But, I have stage 4 lung cancer, and have to begin treatments soon. But, I have a cat. Who's going to take care of my cat, Batou? But. But. But." Jeffery slunked lower in his chair.

"Listen to me, Jeffery, there are challenges here, but none of them insurmountable to you going to Japan."

"What about flying?"

"What are you scared of?"

"Well crashing, of course. And, you know, crashing in the ocean. And then the sharks." Jeffery watched her closely, but not a hint of a smile was betrayed. He thought it silly, but it also seemed logical to him. If you survive the crash in the ocean (which would be bad enough) you have to survive the sharks. "I don't suppose you can just hypnotize me so I can get on the plane?"

"Yes, Jeffery, I think I can."

Jeffery sat up straighter, a smile spreading across his lips. They talked for the rest of the hour, and at the end Jeffery was hopeful.

"Umm…" he began before leaving. "Do you help non-Dream Makers patients?"

She smiled and said, "Yes, I do. I would love to help you with this. Give your insurance information to my assistant and I will have her see if they will cover your visits."

Jeffery Smith's farewell party was held at the dojo. It was, really, the place he felt most at home, the place he felt he most belonged.

He had only planned to go for three weeks; there were still so many uncertainties, and his oncologist was having a fit about him waiting so long to start treatments.

When Sensei had brought up the idea of the party, he had demurred, but Sensei had insisted, telling him, "If the last few weeks has taught us anything Jeffery, it is that life is uncertain. If you don't want to call it a farewell party, call it a celebration of your upcoming adventure."

There were about 15 people in attendance, which surprised and pleased Jeffery. About half were his dojo-mates, three were accountant friends, three were manga/anime friends, and the last was his sister Amy Smith-Warner.

He was touched that she had driven from Dallas to Houston to attend his party. He would be driving to Dallas early in the morning to catch his plane, and could have said goodbye to her then.

Sensei insisted that he and Jeffery do an aikido demonstration. Normally, Jeffery would have refused to do such a thing in front of friends and family, but Jeffery was not feeling normal anymore. So together they demonstrated the fine art of falling down and getting up.

His friends praised his skill, and attested amazement, which felt good. He knew that even after nearly 20 years of practice he was merely adequate, not excellent. But, he thought, perhaps to those who did not know aikido, what they had seen him doing was amazing.

To a person they all congratulated him on his journey, many with a trace of envy. For although he was seriously ill (and some of his friends could only see that) he was doing the kind of thing the many of them had only dreamed of. He was doing something remarkable.

His sister kissed him on her way out and said, "I am proud of you, Jeff."

Jeffery Smith boarded the Boeing 777 with a smile on his lips; happy despite the persistent cough that would not let him forget his illness. The fear that had always stopped him from flying wasn't gone, it still nipped at the edges of his mind, but he had seen himself fly (and survive) so many times now that this seemed almost normal. Completely unremarkable.

The stewardess greeted him with a smile, "Welcome aboard Japan Airlines."

"*Domo arigato.* Glad to be aboard!" Jeffery replied.

As he walked down the aisle people noticed him. Sometimes a quick glance, sometimes a small smile, sometimes a muffled chuckle. Not only did Jeffery not care, he loved it. He was dressed unusually: he wore black aikido gi pants (he knew they would be comfortable for the long flight), and a black t-shirt with the flag of Japan emblazoned on the front.

He settled into his window seat next to Hana Endo, a Japanese native returning home.

"*Ohayo gozaimasu*," he said to her.

It was morning and he knew enough to know that it was the proper greeting, as opposed to more commonly known "*konnichiwa*".

Hana smiled at Jeffery and replied, "Good morning."

Jeffery Smith introduced himself and they chatted amicably until the plane started accelerating down the runway. Then Jeffery gripped the seat, closed his eyes, and used the visualization that Dr. Thompson had taught him. Over and over he saw himself enjoying the flight and safely getting off the plane in Tokyo. He did this until the fear had passed and they were well on their way.

Later, after explaining his quest to Hana, he pulled out the glossy prints he had made of his shogun dream images and showed them to her. At one, a beautiful picture of a Buddhist temple, she said, "I know that one! It is the Fugen-in temple on Mount Koya, and it is *shukubo*."

"*Shukubo?*" Jeffery asked, "What is *shukubo?*"

"They rent rooms to foreigners, you could stay there."

Jeffery Smith spent several delightful days seeing the sites in Tokyo before boarding a train to Osaka. Once in Osaka it took a subway, a train, another subway, a cable car up Mount Koya, a bus, and finally a short walk to get him in front of the Fugen-in temple. He stood there in awe, taking in the grace of the traditional Japanese architecture, the beauty of the finely sculpted topiary, the sweet smell of the cherry blossoms, and the wonders of the delicate gardens. The beauty of it took his breath away and brought tears to his eyes.

He felt transported back in time to 17th century Japan. Just as he first experienced it as a boy with his father watching Shogun.

This was better than movies, or anime, or manga, or even his memory of the temple from his shogun dreams. This was Japan, for real and in person. This was home.

*

Jeffery Smith was deeply troubled as he sat in his small room at the Fugen-in temple. He was meditating, *zanzen* style, as the monks had taught him. His three weeks were at an end, and if he was to return to Houston he must go catch the bus in less than an hour.

He felt death all around him. Death if he returned to Houston; while the radiation treatments might extend his life, what about the quality of his life? Death if he stayed; while the quality of his life might be higher for a time, it would surely be shorter.

He returned his attention to his breath, letting go of his worry yet again. One, inhale; two, exhale; three, inhale. He counted silently, as he had been taught, to help keep his mind from wandering.

But, how could he leave? To his great delight he had discovered that some of the monks practiced aikido, and that Buddhism—which he hadn't seriously studied up until now—dovetailed perfectly with the martial art. How could he leave Mr. Kishi, the gardener, who had so swiftly taught him more about Bonsai than all the books he had read?

One, inhale; two, exhale...

But how could he not return home? There he had insurance that would cover his treatments and make sure he would be cared for at the end, if it came to that. Remarkably he didn't feel much different than when he arrived. The cough was not gone, but it was not any worse. Maybe this lifestyle was changing him; maybe he would live longer here.

One, inhale; two, exhale; three, inhale; four exhale…

And what of longevity? He could die on the walk to the bus, or at any time for that matter. But he couldn't completely abandon himself to the ancient practices, it just didn't seem wise.

One, inhale; two, exhale; three, inhale; four exhale…

His mind finally calmed, he quietly completed his meditation and rose. His path was clear now, he was certain.

∗

Jeffery Smith was a wholly remarkable man. At the age of forty-nine after being diagnosed with stage 4 non-small cell lung cancer, he left Houston and moved to Japan.

He sought refuge in a Buddhist temple on Mount Koya, and there he found his true home. He meditated, practiced aikido, gardened, studied Zen Buddhism, and eventually became a monk.

He combined modern medicine with *Kampo* (Japanese herbal medicine), and a Buddhist lifestyle to dance with his illness. And "dancing" is what he called it. He could not hate, or fight, that which had brought him to his true joy in life. His lung cancer eventually went into remission and he enjoyed many years of good health.

When the tell-tale cough came back at the age of fifty-seven, Jeffery was not scared, merely curious. He went to his oncologist and discovered that the disease had come back, and that it was time to dance with it once again.

Jeffery Smith died a good death several months later at his beloved *Fugen-in* temple.

Jeffery Smith was a wholly remarkable man.

"*futoufukutsu*: No matter what difficulties you encounter,
never let your heart/mind/spirit falter."
Calligraphy by Alon Adika

Butoh In A Stone Garden

a poem by silent lotus

Her

Painted lips

Soft and as ancient

As the tensho that kissed

A seal of silk &

Silence

The

Art of eclipse

Like the last years of Dejima

Bowed with the bamboo

To the wind of the

Shinkansen

A

Night of

Candles and

Noren

Spring

On both sides of

Sliding

Doors

Sendai Space Elevator
a poem by Uche Ogbuji

Fowl flexed paper wings
Leading trains of fleshly birds,
Their silicon brains
Reticulate in sunlight

As we glided up the lift.
Sendai dove below,
Classic lace of green at first
Shifting into reds

And finally royal gold--
Man-made mirage of sunset
We were halfway up
She leaned into the chic bises--

Impulse that shocked me--
Then I felt the nerve-prick glow--
She smiled as I stroked my cheek.
Sudden memory:

The first time I took this ride,
Dusk on the platform…
Not counting the nearby flag,
I watched sunrise twice that day.
I followed suit when
She reached for her power charm

Hung on her necklace--
Three free months of energy

Recharged in the star-shaped pendants.
And perhaps more, shared:
She switched her pupils to zoom
And locked her bright stare

On the silver sphere of her flat
And mine, which might soon be joined.
Our past five miles down,
We stretched out four shape-shift hands

Five miles to future,
Adjusting eye zoom to blue,
To ruby blue and star white.
I closed my eyelids

And thought of Masamune:
Twenty million eyes
Complete his own wonder at
The blue-green-white heights of Sendai.

A Piece in History

flash fiction by Jane Roberts

1690 There is a serpent that lies deep in the heart of the smouldering stone. At the opening of the kiln, it can be heard to roar from the abyss of its expansive belly. The resulting heat bites around the hands and faces of the men removing the pottery. Some believe that the flames blaze out from its fork-tongued mouth, and that must be the reason why the heat prickles and stings even their hardened skin; others know the fire to be a different magic of nature, but still a law unto itself and, therefore, untrustworthy. An inquisitive few are known to have lost their lives, swallowed up in this limbo land between nature and artifice.

Out of the furious *Noborigama* multi-chambered kilns, cloned regiments of pottery outwit the embrace of the serpent and are received into calmer atmospherics; when the pots break, they are forsaken and devoured by the serpent. An improvement upon those ancient fires in earthy ditches, the new *Noborigama* kilns produce far more volume and consistency in one firing than the single-chambered *Anagama* kiln used for ash-glazed pottery. The twenty-four hour age of industry is established; the evergreen countryside is lit up with swarms of paper lanterns and kilns glowing like fire flies in the night air.

Under the illuminated canopies set back from the kilns, each craftsman takes two skeletons of thrown clay and, like a priest at the nuptials of a young couple, marries the separate pieces to create a double-walled vase. On its surface skin the crackling glaze is mottled celadon green and pale blue. The vase is now ready for the **Kanō** artist to bestow upon it a golden gift of artistry. This is the art of Fukushima. This is *Somayaki*.

1978 The hero, a veritable present-day *Minamoto no Yoshitsune*, wields his mighty sword high above his head. He staggers slightly under the weight, as he attempts to cartwheel past a sign which reads: *Somayaki* Vase, late 17th century, Fukushima, N Japan.

As early as the Edo Empire, Soma nobility abetted the construction of many kilns for the mass production of pottery. Later, under the restored power of the Meiji, these armies of kilns would become obsolete. *Somayaki* pottery is much admired, as everyday ware and as fine art. This rare example is believed to date back to the beginning of the trend.

This year, 1978, *Somayaki* pottery has been recognised as one of the national objects of traditional Japanese craftsmanship.

Characteristics of *Somayaki* (Soma Ware): Multi-layered structure. *Ao-hibi*, a crackling effect of the green/blue glaze.

Hashirigoma -- a Kano school of painting stylized galloping horse motif in gold, a tribute to the Fukushima Prefecture's longstanding heritage of equine breeding and training.

This inestimable *Somayaki* vase has watched for nearly three hundred years in a state of blissful inertia as the world and its people have changed around it.

Until today, when Mamoru, the night duty museum curator, has the misfortune to trip over the broom he is wielding as a weapon of mortal combat. Believing the roles to hold similar characteristics of dedicated protection and valiant heart, Mamoru often morphs seamlessly from curator into ancient hero when on the night shift. This is nothing new for the antiquities on display; they are accustomed to his ways.

As he falls onto the display shelf, Mamoru is appalled to realise the vase is ever-so-slightly beyond his grasp. The noble hero finds his body propelled forwards. His chest crashes down on the supported, yet slender, shelf, which snaps like the wishbone of a chicken under his not inconsiderable weight. The vase jumps, an airborne gymnast, graceful, a thing of beauty. It then plummets to the marble floor of the exhibition room, landing clumsily, a thing of great distress to Mamoru.

Spread out on the flecked marble floor, a distracted Mamoru counts 1,393 distorted pieces of history where seconds before only one form of historical perfection existed.

Mamoru is a quick thinker. He recalls a museum visitor that week mocking the Fukushima pottery: "Don't you think it looks like someone has dropped it and stuck it back together with superglue?"

With painstaking sense of duty to his forefathers and the deftness of a child at fault, Mamoru re-pieces each shard and bonds them with glue. Mamoru is fond of jigsaw puzzles and he considers himself strong-willed enough to be up to the challenge. Patience is a virtue of the true warrior. It takes him 7 hours and 23 minutes and 49 seconds to complete his task. He has timed himself just as he would with a jigsaw puzzle.

Setting the patchwork *Somayaki* vase onto a fresh pedestal, he is mystified to discover that one piece -- the tiniest, most miniscule of chips -- remains missing from the base of the vase. Mamoru discards all thoughts of returning to his Samurai sword: this hero's mission has changed. He spends the rest of his shift scanning the marble floor for the missing piece, overlooked by the rising of the Eastern sun, whose effulgent rays lacquer the glass roof of the museum with crimson and catch upon the outline of the revived Kano horse, galloping for eternity in its rustic idyll.

1690 As Kanō Tanshin, artist from the *Kanō* School, glides his brush over the vase, the *Hashirigoma* bolts to life. Finished, the bottom of the vase is chipped when he rests it on the hard stone work table. Kanō Tanshin is horrified to discover the defect, but he comes to the conclusion that he is a perfectionist and no one else will notice such a small chip. Lying unheeded by the feet of the artist is a small fragment of celadon green and pale blue crackle-glazed pottery; piece.

Summer Tofu in Kyoto

a poem by Marianne Betterly

Shafts of rain cannot drown

the scent of cedar incense

or cloud my view

of wooden walls in Gion and

the geisha, still hidden, behind the shoji screen.

A shop has been selling combs

there hundreds of years,

despite three fires

reducing Kyoto to ash.

Near Nanzenji temple

I eat summer tofu--

soft, smooth as silk

floating in a blue bowl

with ice and one red cherry.

Four hundred years ago the bandit Goemon

preferred boiled tofu;

captured by Hideyoshi at the temple's gate,

he admired the beauty of Kyoto

before he was immersed, like tofu,

in bubbling oil.

I think of him as another cool cube, uncooked,

slips down my throat.

The Road to NeoSendai

a story by Donald Jacob Uitvlugt

haru	**spring**
kimi ya chōyou	you the butterfly
ware ya sōshi ga	I the dreaming heart
umegokoro	of Sōshi

-- Matsuo Bashō (1644-1694)

As we travel, I read about the ancients, their beliefs, their thoughts, their dreams. We are going to live like them when we arrive, after all. None of the modern conveniences we had depended on before we left. None of the technology that is tearing our old world apart. A new beginning.

The ancients believed that while we sleep, while we dream, our souls can travel. Taking the form of a butterfly, they roam at will, flitting on the breeze. Once the soul sees what it wished to see, it returns to the body, and the sleeper may never know of its journey. Or perhaps the soul might so enjoy its new, fluttering life that it never returns. The sleeper never wakes up.

I find it hard not to think of that belief when I look out at the solar sails that propel our ship. Great gossamer iridescences, powered by massless protons. Or perhaps by the dreams of all those left behind. Perhaps by the dreams of those strung out in the cryogenic pods behind the colony ship. Perhaps by your dreams. Do you dream of me as I dream of you? Not that I really dream. I do not sleep. The drugs that the needles pump into my system keep me in a state of semi-awareness. The computer takes care of most of the routine maintenance, but it is not so good at improvising. Beside the fact that humans feel better with a fellow human at least metaphorically at the helm.

So the computer wakes me up every three months, has me check the trajectory of the ship, the condition of the cryopods, the trim of the solar sails. The rest of the time I am suspended in a kind of half-sleep, observing all, ready to be awakened in case the computer comes upon an emergency beyond the limits of its programming. The days drag, a life lived at a thousandth of the speed of a normal life. Only the knowledge that you are there keeps me sane. Knowing that at our journey's end, we will build a new world together. We will build a new life together. Knowing that you are dreaming of me as I dream of you…

natsu	summer
botan chirite	fallen peony
uchi kasanarinu	on top of one another
nisanpen	two, three petals

-- Yosa Buson (1716-1783)

The alarms sound. Something is wrong. My eyes open wide as adrenalin and a host of other drugs I don't remember the name of pump into my system. I am alert, already trying to process the information the computer is pumping into me with the drugs.

Two of the sails have collapsed, leaving our ship a wounded butterfly, a crumpled flower. Ordinarily this would not be a problem. The computer would analyze the situation, send out the repair bots on the scaffolding, and the bots would spin new sails.

But for some reason, the repair bots are not responding to the computer's signals. So it wakes me, puts me into a heightened state of awareness. I realize that I cannot do anything without information, so I jack myself directly into the computer.

The data are overwhelming. I am the ship, kilometers long, wings hundreds of kilometers across. I know the name of each of the occupants of the cryopods, what their occupations will be on NeoSendai, their psychological profiles, why they enlisted for this one-way voyage. I see you. The sight calms me, gives me the strength to swim where I need to in the sea of data.

I see the issue now. A micro-asteroid has hit the control node for one of the sails. The repair bots happened to be docked there at the same time. A freak accident, but one the computer is not programmed to handle. I am almost aware of the computer in my consciousness. It is like a lost, frightened child. The port connecting us is like the clasp of hands.

I wonder how it will feel to hold the hand of one of our children. The collapsed sails put us off course. A matter of a few degrees, but when the journey is measured in light years, a small deviation is the difference between reaching our destination and eternally sailing the void of space. The computer cannot correct the course. The ruined sails interfere. I make the decision to blow them.

The slightest of tremors, like the flutter of butterfly wings or the petals of a flower in the summer breeze. And then we are beyond them, leaving them behind like a shed skin. I attempt the course correction again. We inch closer, but still do not fly true. I know what has to be done, and my slowed heart thuds in my chest. I have to go outside and fix the sails.

Aki	fall
utsukushi ya	how lovely
shōji no ana no	through the torn paper screen
amanogawa	the river of heaven

-- Kobayashi Issa (1763-1827)

Everything seems distorted. There is no true sense of scale, thanks to the time-dilating drugs. It takes me a day to disconnect the feeding and waste removal tubes, the monitoring leads, the cortical umbilicus to the computer. I disconnect from the computer last. It feels so small to be only myself again.

I consider giving myself a metabolism boost. But there is a long journey yet ahead of us. Mess with my metabolism too much and my life will burn out before we reach our destination. I want to be there to welcome you to our new home.

If my repairs fail, the ship will sail until the sensors find a sun promising a life-bearing planet. Or it will simply drift until the ship systems fail one by one. Our entire journey will have been a dream from which you never wake up.

I cannot bear that thought. It takes a week to pull and test the new bot node from the stores, another week to put on the EVA suit. At times I have to remind myself to breathe, to blink. The computer would have helped me remember, but I forget to set the reminders before I disconnect. I do not have time to plug back in and set them. The airlock cycles in the blink of an eye. I must be careful, must be deliberate. The laws of physics are not changed, only my reaction time to them. I make sure the new node is clipped to my belt, that my tether is clipped right outside the hull door. I press the release.

The ship accelerates away from me. I have just enough zero-gee training not to be sick. I expect space to be cold around me, but I feel only the humming warmth of the EVA suit.

The ship floats below me. Below? Does it matter? I choose the ship as a point of reference, I choose for it to matter. Thus it is below me, no longer a butterfly or flower, but a dragonfly, long body and shiny wings. A dragonfly from which some cruel cosmic child has torn a pair of wings. Wings that I will re-attach in an anti-entropic feat of magic.

Time disappears. I play out the tether cable, days, weeks, months. I do not know. Through the two great tears in the solar sails, I see the stars. Some think of space as cold and devoid of live. Heartless. This moment, I know that thought to be a lie. The ancients were right to see the galaxy as heaven's river. The flow of life is intimately connected to the flux of the stars. If we do not hear the heartbeat of the starts, perhaps it is only because we do not listen hard enough.

Or perhaps it is because we ourselves are that heart beat. A few pulses of the EVA jets and I reach the hub at last, where ship and sails connect. I see the damaged unit immediately. The ship's design is modular. I have only to eject the old unit and replace it with the new one.

The locks burst in a puff of gas, but the damaged node stays put. I frown and maneuver my body over it. I tug the node free. I go flying with it, spinning out into space. I am spinning too fast. I black out…

fuyu   **winter**

kangetsu ya   winter moonlight
sekitō no kage   shadow of the stone pagoda
matsu no kage   shadow of the pine

-- Masaoka Shiki (1867-1902)

An alarm wakes me again. Different than the computer's alarm. It is closer, yet somehow more distant. I open my eyes. It is dark. I do not know where I am at first. I am dying. Perhaps I am already dead and I will never see your face again.

The alarm is insistent. It calls me back to reality. This is the alarm the EVA suit uses to tell its user there is less than a third of his air left. I sink into despair. Even if I can figure out where I am, even if I can find the ship, I do not have time to complete my task. I will die, and you will sleep in the void forever.

Still it is dark. I realize in an instant where I am. I have drifted under the ship. I float in the shadows created by the lights that shine on the sails to help me in my task. I press the button on my tether line. If the line is not tangled, it will pull me back to the airlock door. A small comfort, your body inside its cryopod, mine outside the ship, but united in their unfulfilled dreams.

I should not have left the safety of my chair. Should have found another way around the problem. Or even if I could not have divined another solution, I could have lived out the remainder of my extended life connected to you through the computer link.

The solution comes to me then, in the midst of my despair. A glowing moon shining in the night. The EVA suit is designed for use near Earth. It was never thought I would have to use it. It was never recalibrated for my slowed metabolism. I may have all the air I need.

I reel myself in along the tether, making sure that the bot node is still firmly on my belt. Eons of non-time pass, but I smile. A laugh echoes in my heart. At last I reach the hub again. The waiting socket embraces the node like a lover. As you will welcome me when we reach our new home. The node powers up, a small lantern shining into the night. Bots crawl from it and begin to spin new gossamer sails.

I laugh aloud this time, though no one can hear me. I begin the long journey back to the ship, and I think of you. I think of our new home. I think of our life together. And I smile.

Japanese Arts
a poem by Annie Gustin

haiku--

a few words will do.

pen poised on paper,

seventeen syllables--a skeleton

the reader clothes with her mind

coloring in the photograph

the poet left behind.

the painting--

a handful of brushstrokes will suffice

to capture the wind, the snow,

the fractured ice

    delicate branches against the blue

    a pained expression

    across her lips--one stroke

    for her eyebrows—two.

samurai sword--

sheath, swoop, sheath

his life for his lord

    a scribble in the breeze

    blink of an eye

    the samurai rests

    blade shimmering nearby.

hair sticks cross at her nape

a taiko drummer lifts his arm

chopsticks between fingers

a sensei's staff--first, do no harm…

hiragana, katakana

sweeps of ink, paper-thin

…brush, pen, swords

a few strokes will do

to express the spirit

within.

Origami

flash fiction by Jen Campbell

We used to make paper aeroplanes at school, but those weren't good enough. Now I spend my weekends practising the art of folding into myself, examining my nose in the mirror: the arch of it, the length, the pliability. I take a crayon to my eye sockets and paint the dark outlines of cranes. The cranes I used to fold for tables at the restaurant down the road. In three months I made just over five hundred. They were in several colours, their necks resting on each other, asleep. Me: I can strip down to be any colour I like. With folding paper, one side of it is always immaculate and decorated, like the inside of my skin. Inside here, you can feel it. I sharpen my finger nails with paper cuts, take off my shoes and put my feet in the mud, stretching out my hands to see if, on one side, I can touch the summer house and, on the other, the tree by the gatepost. I cannot quite make it yet, stretching so far my skin might snap. Feathers are itching their way out under my nails. I bend down and touch my toes, try to look out sideways. There are five hundred more cranes to go. When I can extend that far, I am ready to fly.

City Stories

Ninja
flash fiction by Kyle Hemmings

I wake up with a scream. Mine. On the pillow next to me, Zin opens one eye then the other. When did you shave your head? I ask.

Oh, some guy crept in last night and cut it. I think he was a modern ninja. He said he wanted to bring my chestnut locks to his master. His master thought chestnut was just for horses. There might be a ritual involved. Maybe even barter. My lock for seven of your dribbling goats that you promised could talk like big shit mountain gods. I couldn't see much of him in the dark, but he was kind of cute dressed as a simple wood gatherer. Then he flew out the window like a skylark. Or maybe the floor opened up for him. I bet he could walk on water too. Maybe surf on a wave of my hair. I don't think it was a dream.

Very funny, I say.

I dive head first under the sheets. I'm Jacques Cousteau without a flashlight, looking for signs of hair.

Stop, Zin says, that tickles.

I'm on a mission, I say, just hold your breath.

You feel like a water spider.

How would you know what a water spider feels like?

A ninja crept into my room last night.

She catches my head in a leg scissors and says for me to say Ninja Uncle. Instead, I bite into her flesh that only remotely tastes like a soft salt pretzel.

You suck, monster, she says, muff diver, lowboy. My ninja man would never bite me. If he knew, he'd kill you with a dart. Avenge my dishonor.

In black bra and panties, Zin walks across the floor with soft even foot-slaps. She opens the window and yells out over Avenue C: Anybody see my Water Spider Man? He got away with my hair.

I get dressed and turn on Canadian radio. A news report about a hiker, stranded in the wilderness for weeks, claiming to have lived on fly soup and bear paw. Returning home, he couldn't adjust to society and, last seen, he was walking naked along a highway.

Do you think he was kidnapped by a bear? I ask Zin.

Oh God, she says, I got blood on my panties. Those cramps last night hurt. Like worse than the worst. Made me crazy.

So, like you got crazy and like cut your own hair?

I said like those cramps hurt. Most people listen with only ¼ of their brain. With you, it stops at the ear canal and turns to wax.

Take some Black Haw. It's good for cramps.

You speak from experience?

My ex, who loved listening to Insects in Minor Keys, said it worked.

Was she a grasshopper?

No, Aquarius. She was from South London.

Go to England and suck breast milk.

It's too far and I can't swim.

Well, I can't feed you today. I'm all out of milk and somebody took my hair. Maybe tomorrow.

A promise?

Sure, monster.

Zin fixes me with one of her wistful glares, half-blue and half-me. The growing smile, homemade, made of so many holes, blood-fits, and needle-pricks. Her gift to me.

We spend the rest of the morning, chasing and hugging each other's shadow, waiting for the ninja to return.

Ueno Park

a poem by Jonathan Greenhause

An egret balances upon
a wooden stake half-sunk into the pond
    where a dozen swan
-shaped rowboats glide across its surface,

& two ducks
swim in-sync by the stake, their
    beaks
dipping into water, emerging &

submerging meticulously-preened feathers
    & circling around the egret
before returning from whence they came,
    into the embrace
of a weeping willow's drooping leaves.

An old man stands
at the pond's soggy edge, tossing
    shredded bread,
as gigantic carp tussle for it, their cavernous mouths
    swallowing it whole

as the turtles grasp what they can
because of the man's compassion
    & impeccable aim,

while from a bandstand,
a woman sings a jazz standard,
    by a pond
filled with lotuses,

their intense perfume pervading
    everything
& reaching me on this bench
    as I take in
all these tiny miracles.

What is freedom?

An excerpt from the novel Dog Mountain by Iain Maloney

Freedom is the passenger seat of a black Toyota van, empty coffee cans rolling around your feet. Two surfboards in the back; the sun hours from rising. A new pipe bought in Osu Kannon, the air sweet with Hokkaido Homegrown, the road empty, the speed needle in the hundreds and a beach waiting for you and at the end of the beach, the ocean.

Exodus. On a 3am highway on an August morning the world is split into truckers and surfers. Movement of ja people. We're all driving to get somewhere. We know where we're going. Machines buzz, workers toil, clock in, clock out; we slip south to Toyohashi just factories, factories, immigrant workers, all night bars and the Pacific clawing the coast. Freedom is entropy; entropy freedom. We're jamming, jamming until the jamming is through. We hope you like jamming too.

Hitoshi hits my shoulder says duuuude. Hitoshi's favourite movie is The Big Lebowski. People think he can speak English, but all he knows are Big Lebowski lines. He reckons he can cover most conversational situations with any foreigner that way. Dude. I take a last quick blast, hand the pipe over, skip Turn Your Lights Down Low because it's just me and Hitoshi, and he's my best mate but I don't want to sit in the dark singing I want to give you some good good lovin'. Skip. Don't worry about a thing, coz every little thing's gonna be alright.

Pipe back. Van returns to its lane, hands back on the wheel.

You found Tuesday yet? he asks.

No. No idea.

Worried?

Not today.

And I'm not. This is a holiday from life. Get high and surf. Jammin'

Heard from Mai?

Nothing.

No woman. No cry.

You hear me crying?

I hear your heart breaking. She's a good girl. Get her back.

Should I take advice from you?

You take drugs from me. Why draw a line?

Good point. Any food left?

There's a chip under the brake pedal.

I'm good.

Unemployment opens time. Instead of rising at nine and wasting the summer in a swivel chair selling fashion masquerading as communication I can stay up all night, road trip and use what's left of the summer as it was meant to be used. Toiling through school summers, mountains of homework and revision for the test first day back - not that I did any of it but I wasn't allowed to leave the table until I'd put in a full shift - I came to respect the raw draw of summer heat, the animal need to be outside, and the soul sickness that results from imprisonment. I have a habit of losing jobs around the end of the rainy season. Pure coincidence.

Hitoshi updates me with news from world of phones. Nakata has now decided that in order to save some money, air conditioning will only be used in customer areas. In the depths of August, this is proving unpopular with the workforce, who have responded with a series of 'work-to-rule' protests. Hitoshi cultivates a dead sweat smell and then stays as close to Nakata as he can, only just stopping short of hugging him. Keiko is coming to work in increasingly casual and revealing clothes, which has the triple benefit of keeping her cool, increasing her ability to sell phones to male customers and of making Nakata hot enough to retire somewhere private where there's no air con.

Normality is soothing, if you can call time spent with Hitoshi normal. He's not trying to find doors to other dimensions, nor seeking mystical worlds under his doorstep. I've said it before, and I'll say it again: there's something wrong with the baby boom generation. I'm going to restrict my social life to anyone who can't remember the Sixties because they weren't there.

How can one generation be so schizophrenic? The Beatles, hippy, free love and drugs, student protests, street violence and an exploding left wing grew into amoral conservatives, hypocrites espousing humanism while exploiting, grabbing everything they could get their hands on. Flooding the seas with cyanides while singing Imagine at exclusive karaoke bars. Strip-mining Japan physically and metaphysically. Ito played bass in a psychedelic band. My father was behind the barricades. My father, now at the centre of the right wing elite, stood with Baba Rie, a woman who carried Mao's Little Red Book as religiously as Mai carries her make up case. It turns out The Beatle they were most like was Yoko Ono.

Still, they'll be gone soon, and then we can set about changing the world. Where would we be without mortality?

I see the sea as the sea sees me. We crest the hill with the bang of surfboards on the roof and there she is, Pacific-chan. Squeal of breaks and into the convenience store, piss, stock up on supplies, smokes and rice balls. Old guy behind the counter doesn't like us with our youth and hair and lack of respect, but loneliness is stronger than disapproval.

Going surfing?

Yeah uncle. Coming?

Typhoon coming.

Big waves.

Dangerous.

Dangerous, Hitoshi agrees.

I nod, sage-like.

We bid him long life and prosperity, empty the empties from the van into his bins, ignoring the recycle segregation. I sniff the air: ocean. Salt. Storm coming. Hitoshi burps.

Hurry up Dude. Sea's getting cold.

Don't worry. The waves won't start without us.

Yeah, but all the good girls will be gone.

I don't want the good girls. I want the bad girls.

He guns the gas and we lurch onto the road, follow gravity to the edge.

Bob finishes, One Love / People Get Ready; people are ready Bob, ready and waiting.

What'll we have?

Beach Boys. Surf music. Give us some Pet Sounds, dude.

No chance. Piss weak music. We need something with a BEAT. Eastern Youth.

Punk? After Bob? No chance.

We agree on Mothercoat, Patchwork-shiki. Drums vibrating speakers, slap dashboard and wheel. Went to see them in Shin-Sakae in the spring, a few bands, bit of a mix, punk, post-rock, electronica. Mothercoat headlined and killed competition dead. Meanest drummer I've ever seen, all arms and legs and hair, a blur of rhythm. Was my Dad like that? Hard to imagine him drumming, smooooooooth jazz brush strokes, rolls up rolls down, cigarette in the corner of his mouth, sweat pouring down back and front, all cool and smoky in Shinjuku. Whenever the stereo went on at home it was jazz vinyl, all crackly yeahs and huhs and bangs and hoots, Yamashita Yosuke mostly. Guess he knew him, maybe even played together.

All those records. I used to love flicking through them while he was out, the huge sleeves, every inch artwork. These skinny black guys in sharp suits. Art Blakey grinning at the drums in yellow wash. John Coltrane looking pensive, thoughtful in Blue Train blue. Abstract monochrome of Dancing Kojiki, Yamashita Yosuke live in '69. He'd have beaten me for touching them, if he knew. They were like holy relics, mementos of a previous life, which I guess they were. He gave it all up to follow his father who followed Sato onto a plane to America. Maybe he'd have made records if he'd chosen Shinjuku over the establishment. Surely more a piece of his soul than the Immigration Control Act or the Health and Safety legislation that bears his name.

Will I ever do anything worth leaving behind? My personality still tangible once I'm gone? The Tale of Nomura. What would my artefact be? I can't paint, write, make music. I can't change the world; I can't change anything. A footnote in a political biography. Son of. Grandson of. Brother of. Uncle of. Is there anything I can do? What do I want to do? Do I want to do anything?

Who's John Perry? Hitoshi asks.

No idea. Why?

She's singing about him. He nods at the stereo. Says John Perry called her a bitch.

Maybe ex-boyfriend.

I'd like to be her ex-boyfriend. She was hot.

Probably still is. I don't think I'd like to be her ex-boyfriend. Not if she was then gonna write a song about me.

I'd like someone to write a song about me.

One that lists everything bad about you?

That'd be a short song.

He starts singing. I love you Hitoshi, you're just so fucking cool, I love you Hitoshi, please meet me after school.

You want to watch that fascination with school girls. It'll get you in trouble one day.

Lots of things'll get me in trouble one day, until then, where's that pipe gone?

It's hard to think about your problems when an ocean is trying to kill you. The storm waves are high and vicious, rolling long and hard. The sea is grey, the breakers white, mad. One foot wrong and you're face down with a breaking back. There's a better beach around the headland, but it's more populous, and we're in no state to be weaving. Mary Jane on the brain, thoughts fluid, the dawn sea washing me clean. This is what I need.

I push the board, feeling the pull of the water, the currents rushing, and carve a route along the curling wave, balancing along the horizon where pressure and gravity meet, the edge of forces. Out at sea the typhoon is spinning, whipping up a rage, lifting the Pacific and throwing it back down. We play on the boundaries, bravely mocking, staying where we can see danger, where it can't touch us. We're too flimsy to approach.

Out of shape, I feel the strain, tension in the thighs and calves, give up, but it's hard to leave the water, the ebb curling my ankles, drawing me back, the one more wave. Wipes me out, wade to shore and stretch out on the sand, sheltered from the wind by tank blocks, seventy years old, still waiting. The sky is beautiful, chased clouds catching the dawn red, darker and deeper at the horizon. It'll hit by tonight, no escape. Trawlers are moving in, nets drifting through the breakers. Storm must be welcome to them. A day off, lie in bed. Sake evening without worrying about the morning.

A day in bed. Doze awake, Mai on my chest, breasts pressed against. Have a smoke, fumble for remotes and get the music going, something ambient to bring in the light, Marihiko Hara maybe, nudge her with my erection until she gets the hint. Arguing over who's going to the convenience store for breakfast, even though it's always me. Watch DVDs until the energy bubbles up and we have to get outside, go to the mall or the games centre, Italian buffet for dinner. Couple of drinks, home for sex on the sofa and whatever's on TV.

I should go and see her again. Sort this out. That, at least, is something I can do, an action I can take. It'd be nice to talk to someone who understands me. I'll show her *The Tale Of Matsui*. I think she'd like it. She likes those myths of old, the tales from the Heian-era and before. If I'd read it before the meeting with my father I'd have thought no more about it than that. Now, I'm not sure. Obviously they found this Dog Mountain, or at least that's what Baba Rie, my father and Ito Kaisuke think. What's stranger is the similarity with Honda's story about his monk. Living in a cave, disappearing. Is any of this true? There are too many coincidences, too many possibilities, too many things that could be true and important, or irrelevant and false. All I want is to find out why I lost a day and get my girlfriend back, the rest can go hang. To be honest, I'm not even sure I care about the lost day. Finding out won't give me the time back, or my job, so what's the point?

No, stop. Clear mind, look at the clouds, listen to the waves. Close eyes and sink. I drop my defences and let sleep come. Sink.

The Hankyu Line

a poem by Elizabeth Schultz

Young lovers muse
on each other's palms.
Sloppy businessmen
sprawl over seats.
Plugged in students nod.

For half an hour
we share a common
direction and destiny.
Station by station,
they change, move on.

Only the woman,
brushing her teeth
over an orange basin,
is framed forever
in the train window

As I look directly
into her room
at the Nakatsu stop.

This Space
haibun by Mark Kerstetter

The planned and the serendipitous go together in this cube of air, and the weather's blindfold can do no additional harm in the night of night. Our job is to grope toward a form in what is quickly becoming a free-fall zone. This is the moment one learns to transform the blind outward thrust into a discrete gesture. It's just survival, but it can be more, as Alice returning from her adventure pours the rain into a pantomime not yet deciphered amidst the tinkling teacups.

the space between

swirling cherry blossoms

margin of marvels

Walking on Roofs
flash fiction by Adnan Mahmutović

My name is Niels Bohr. I was born in 1885, on a cold night, and I fell in love with heat. I liked pressing my fingertips to warm windowpanes, my wife's lips, lake pebbles outside my cabin, invisible grains of dust that shine up in the air.

Now I like to walk on roofs. When I first started in 1945, I was light as a candle flame. Unbearably light. I moved with ease of a sparrow with an olive leaf in its beak. I had the leg power of a stork that brings children to happy parents, and the mind of a raven. Powerful enough to play with atoms.

It is 2011 and I'm old now. Too old to be jumping from rooftop to rooftop in this Japanese village. Too old and too scared to go down to earth.

My fingers hurt when I lift a few decayed tiles and peer into the attic. Streetlight stirs dust. I don't go in. I don't sleep in other people's houses any longer. I snug up to smokeless chimneys on warm nights, or cringe close to the weathercocks.

I take no pleasure in watching nighttime tragedies and comedies of existence. I'm not a voyeur. I fall in love every night, at dusk and dawn, with beautiful mothers and fathers, sons and daughters, solitary streetwalkers, cats and mongrels, rats which never sleep, moths tangled in gossamer staring at candles in the windows.

Tonight my one hundred and twenty-five years old feet hurt against the fragile roofs of this new village. It feels like it was yesterday I scurried the flat tops of New York.

The tiles are like glass dust.

I lie down on my stomach, my head hanging over the roof edge. The light in the room underneath is weak. A boy and a girl, twins, are watching a broken TV screen. I cannot hear sounds, but they may be talking. The girl's stiff fingers barely touch her brother's crew cut hair. To his left there is a mask of a Samurai.

I tilt my head back and forth, trying to see who else is in the

156

house. A dark-haired woman leans on the kitchen door frame, smiling coyly at the bulky man doing yoga on the floor. Her heel is high up in the air. His four fingertips touch the tips of her toes, lifting them up from the floor linoleum, her thumb the only part of her delicate foot still pressed against the floor, as if he is trying to help her do a pirouette. They are stuck in that intimate gesture. There is no further movement. She is not a ticklish subject to his tickling experiment with her sole.

I hitch myself up and look over the village. Cats and mongrels, rats and nightingales, yes, they're all there. But they are all too silent, too sleepy, too lazy, hunched close to backyard fences and neatly parked cars. I must have gone deaf. I hear no sounds whatsoever, not even the desert wind. The air is uncannily calm. The trees are petrified.

I spy through more windows. In the smallest house, seven children sit in a circle around a huge bowl of cornbread crumbled and drenched in milk. A father sits hunched in a corner crying, his palms pressed against his eyeballs. The mother is probably in the kitchen.

Across the street, a man and a woman are stuck in the missionary position, their faces distorted with the painful pleasures.

In the largest house with three windows, a boy yells at his brother, who holds his Iron Man toy high in the air threatening to break its left leg. In the third room their grandma is kissing a picture of a handsome mustachioed man in a turban.

For the first time I jump down on the ground. The asphalt is cold. Temperature drops like Newton's infamous apple. I never thought of that, does the gravity affect temperature? How about human warmth?

I walk the empty streets like a straggler. Water runs down the street and splashes at my toes like small rocks. At the edge of the town, the sun is coming up patiently. Still, it's the break of the day. This light is intense, immaculate, warm. The cloud at the horizon does not shield me from the dawn. I put my hands in the air as if to press my fingertips against the hot dusty wind. I glimpse a wall of dark water.

Japanese Bottle by Sharon Ratheiser
(ink on paper collage)

Over Narita
haiku by Brigita Orel

over Narita

we dip into clouds like lips

in cappuccino.

Blue Hearts
flash fiction by Kyle Hemmings

Whenever Beatle-Boy and Zin get into an argument, he will tear his pillows with a *Shonen* knife. He will threaten to love only Tokyo girls, ones who resemble his animations. Or he will sleep under the house with the goat-boys, made homeless under the city's new urban renewal program. They are dreamless and have no sense of mute beat. If things get too heated, Beatle-Boy will get lost in L-shaped rooms under streets and gear-grind, doing the Trip Hop before hookers having ticks and herniated discs. When he returns home, he will be in a trance. For days, all doors will be closed. But Zin being a girl-rapper trained in classical, will stand in the rain. This is not to say that every time Zin and Beatle-Boy argue, there will be rain. The rain is not logical, and contrary to popular opinion, has no musical sense. The rain does not say Take off your hi-hat and dance with me. The rain may not be there at all. It's just that in the absence of the other, Zin loves to stand in the middle of a street, oblivious to sky peddlers and pimps on parole. She will throw her head back and open her mouth. She'll convince herself that it's pouring--it's there. She loves the taste of reflexive clouds, an ethereal sadness that is her own.

Kyoto Moss
a poem by silent lotus

In
A lost
Kyoto garden
Our paths crossed
i was waiting for sunrise
And then wind whispers
Cherry blossoms are
As tender as
Moss

Silver Lining
flash fiction by Ida Černe

Spring had finally come, a ripe green spring soaking up the chaos of the previous weeks. I sat on a bench eating a *satsuma* tangerine. Amidst the unravelling of destruction, people were back to doing normal things. The parks were full. Many practiced tai chi there, jogged, or sat on benches reading books. Every once in a while I'd even catch sight of someone doing origami. I was allergic to origami. It was like math. You had to line everything up right. When I was eight or nine, my *Obaachan*, my father's mother who came to live with us after the Kobe earthquake, would fold the small sheets with me.

"Look Hiroko, the legs are too small," she said and put down the green figure.

"Oh, my frog has the right sized legs 3/4 but they're dangling in the wrong direction!" I told her.

"Let's trade," Obaachan suggested.

We switched frogs and tried to unfold the paper mysteries of lower extremities. It was pointless. I left the unfinished frog on the table and walked over to the window to let the sun warm my face.

It wasn't that I lacked patience; I would try and try again. And Obaachan always managed to get our origami into the right shape. She was good with her hands. She could peel a whole tangerine in one long spiral. I often played with that peel. Obaachan told me to throw it on the ground.

"See the character it makes, that will be the shape of your future husband's name," she said.

Obaachan was very old-fashioned, and I thought the game was silly, but it was better than doing homework, better than origami.

"See Hiroko, it looks like 大 3/4 so expect to marry Daichi (大地), Daiki (大輝) or Daisuke (大輔)," she announced.

I preferred the name Takeo (丈夫) so I nudged the peel just a

little with my toe and told her coyly, "I think it's 丈 3/4 丈 for Takeo."

Her expression eased into the wrinkles of her face. She shook her head and wiped her hands on the checkered red apron with an embroidered rooster on it.

"Yes, child, I think you're right. Now that I look closely, it does look like 丈. My future grandson-in-law will be Takeo. He will make you a good husband."

And we would laugh and sip our tea.

Obaachan's hands smelled like tangerines and rice, her apron soaked in scents of the vegetables she chopped so carefully, a grin that filled out her cheeks like *gyoza*. Her quiet smile always kept a secret. But it was spring again, and although I was 16 when she died, five years ago, I often feel her presence like a shadow in my life. Like an empty fullness.

As the sun sank behind me, my shadow threw a shape just like Obaachan hunched over a cup, gently pouring out the tea. I moved forward on the bench. Obaachan moved. Forward. Back. Pouring tea. Pulling back. I leaned back into the heat-filled wood. I saw a young man with a briefcase approach my bench. He sat down at the other end.

He pulled out a crisp newspaper and was soon enfolded in it. I could not peek at the front page. I had seen too many front pages lately. Obaachan had often told me to rest my eyes on greenness. The fresh budding greenery bit into my senses, stinging my eyes, tickling my nose. I looked down to see what I had been nudging with my foot. A discarded cigarette pack. Usually, this park never has litter. I picked it up. I dropped it back to the ground. I pick it up again, meaning to drop it in the garbage on my way home. I could use it to stuff my tangerine peels in. I looked inside. A gleam of sliver. I pulled out the lining. My fingers had a memory all their own. They were folding the paper: points to the middle, fold, turn... I laughed out loud. The man lowered his paper, for a second, to look at what I was doing.

My fingers knew the comfort of folded lines, of neat little edges that ended in points. Was I making a frog or a crane? I made precise folds. I made order. Giving a simple sheet of paper a shape, a purpose. Soon I was at the inverse folds and the points stayed stubbornly tucked in. After the third attempt, I flattened it all out. I let out a heavy sigh, and laid the intact slip of paper down on the bench.

Now, the man put down his newspaper. Calmly, he picked up the silver lining and looked at me. I nodded. He smoothed out the paper, then he spilt it down the middle. He gave me one half of the paper to hold, while he tore the second half into four perfect squares. As he handed me one of the small squares, his fingers brushed mine. Then, he began to fold, shaping the square into a boat-shaped strip. I copied each of his steps, carefully; then set down my finished strip, a boat-shaped form, next to his three identical ones. The other half, the long strip, he rolled into what looked like a stem. Smiling shyly, he slowly looped the stem over three small strips and twisted them into position. He put in a fourth strip in and twisted the paper down to the bottom of the stem. After plucking the silver blossoms open, one by one, turning down each point, and smoothing it out, he held the flower with both hands, and stood and bowed formally as he offered it to me.

I could smell the traces of tangerine on my fingertips, and knew his name before he even spoke a word.

Dance, Journey
haiku by Michelle Goode

sweat trickles over

bubblegum popping lips as

karaoke beats

neon glow passing

memory flash boxed within

shinkansen whispers

Steps and Bows in Tokyo
a poem by Marianne Betterly

a day of a thousand steps

down subterranean stairs, bright tunnels, thru snapping doors;

my teenage son and I sit silently on the subway

in a line of glazed Tokyo commuters

whose same shoes, soft thoughts, semi-closed lullaby eyes

make us feel like the strangers we are,

the only blonds on the train--

no one really stares but

the silence keeps getting louder

as I try to understand the metro map;

the only poster I can read has no words,

warns against speaking on cell phones,

how conversations might make a stranger cry

we wander on narrow Harajuku streets

where girls wobble in three inch gladiator shoes, pink maid frills,

bright red hair,

boys cluster, hollow-cheek lean, jagged bangs waterfall over their eyes,

a rich woman pushes a baby carriage --

inside: a Chihuahua dressed in pink ruffles and bows

night drops around us like a thunder burst;

we return to the alleyways of Asakasa mall, hungry for sushi --

this one has sushi on boats

thank god I can read kanji numbers

stacks of plates later

our bill is somehow less than dinner in Berkeley

the mall is covered in pink paper sakura,

hundreds of stalls sell kimonos, cameras, chopsticks, ceramic bowls

I keep finding things I would have bought for him

if I wasn't his widow--

a little past ten, most shops closed except for pachinko;

as we pass the sushi boat restaurant again,

the chef and two waitress come outside,

bow to us as if honored guests --

we wave, and when we turn the corner, look back --

a second bow, deeper,

warms me like a sip of shochu before goodnight

The Poetry Game
a story by Sessha Batto

"My lover whispers to me."

Kenji recoiled slightly, breaking their tenuous connection and drawing the regard of a passing *maiko*. He watched in growing horror as her eyes raked knowingly over them. She tilted her head, studying the way their shoulders pressed together, then hid her smirk demurely behind her fan and continued on. "Why are you doing this?"

"It's just a game," Ryuu insisted, never taking his eyes off the water flowing beneath their perch. "Afraid to play a simple word game with your best friend?"

"People are watching us." Kenji's face flamed even brighter and he dipped his head to hide his embarrassment while he fought to control his emotions.

"And you're making sure they keep watching. Now concentrate, we're playing the poetry game. I'll start." Tickle of dry lips against a flushed cheek. "My lover whispers to me."

"There must be a better way to spend our last hours together." Kenji ignored the glare directed his way and continued, voice hoarse with unshed tears. "You can't expect me to pretend I'm happy and not say anything, just to make it easier for you."

Ryuu counted to ten in his head, tamping down on his frustration in hopes of salvaging the evening. "Look at me." Strong fingers brushed a tear off a porcelain cheek. "You knew this was coming. I never gave you any indication otherwise."

"Of course. How ridiculous of me to expect the man who shared my bed every night for the last four years would want to stay with me," Kenji hissed. "I should have guessed you were planning on getting married to your high school sweetheart right after graduation."

"Yes, you should have. You know my parents, you should understand the kind of pressure I'm under." Ryuu pulled his lover tight, hands automatically rubbing comforting circles across broad shoulders. "Besides, nothing needs to change. Junko knows how close

168

we are. She'll expect us to spend time together. After all, she's been very patient with me about us."

"She's been patient." The total absence of intonation was a sign of just how far Kenji had shut down. "Well, there's no reason to put her out any longer. I certainly don't see the need to subject myself to any further humiliation." He began struggling, forcing his arms up and pushing his taller lover away. "If you do this our friendship ends. I won't punish myself with your happiness."

"Who says I'm happy? Life isn't about being happy. I don't see you shirking your duty and dishonoring your family."

"Actually, I told them about us last year." Ryuu's eyes widened in shock, he never expected his timid lover would take a stand where his family was concerned. "Of course, you were too busy hiding your engagement from me to notice they haven't called."

"I...why would you do something so stupid?"

Ryuu's words broke the barrier holding his anger at bay. "Stupid? I'm stupid? What about all the promises you made? You told me we'd pledge our commitment under the *sakura* trees in the spring." Despite all that had happened Kenji refused to believe the man he loved would be so carelessly hurtful. That conversation had convinced him to tell his parents about his lover, secure in the knowledge that they would deal with the consequences together.

"I was drunk. Of course I'd tell you what you wanted to hear, what I wish were true, pretty lies and pipe dreams." Ryuu leaned further over the railing, scattering food for the *koi* lurking under the bridge.

"I see. So I'm some simple-minded fool who needs to be lied to?" Kenji flipped from passive to aggressive, abandoning any concern for his supposed friend's feelings. "You are nothing more than a self-centered, egotistical, arrogant, pain in my ass. I'm happy to be rid of you."

"If you really meant that you wouldn't be crying," Ryuu pointed out. "Please don't ruin what's left of the evening. I don't want to leave you like this. I want us to remember this night for the rest of our lives."

Kenji whipped around, clenching the railing until his knuckles bled white. "You can remember what you like. I just want to forget this night as soon as humanly possible." He took a deep breath, forcing his voice to remain steady. "I'm leaving now. Please don't come back to the apartment tonight. I promise I'll make myself scarce tomorrow so you can move your things out."

He started to walk away, but jerked back when a hand caught his wrist in an iron grip. "Don't you dare walk away from me." Ryuu's voice wavered, and he ran a hand over his face as he struggled to control his emotions. "I know it's not what you want, but we can have a good life like this. It isn't easy for me either and I'm counting on you to be there for all the formalities. If you aren't next to me I don't know if I can go through with this farce."

"So, you need to rub my face in it for satisfaction?" The bitterly resigned bite of his words left Kenji's lover wincing.

"No, I need your support to help me do what is right...even though it's not what I want." Ryuu gathered Kenji close, kissing the tip of his nose, then leaning in to touch foreheads. "You are my light. I don't think I can stand living in the dark." They stood like that for some time, wrapped in each other's arms and lost in their thoughts.

"Have you even considered what it will be like for me? I'm not you, I can't manage two separate lives. Most of the time I'll be alone. I don't know if I can stand that."

"I'm a selfish bastard," Ryuu admitted. "I'm asking more of you than I have the right to. But, couldn't we at least try? If it doesn't work for you . . . I want to make it work for you."

"I honestly don't know if that's even possible." Kenji was trying to conceive of a scenario in which he could stay with the man he loved and still be able to look himself in the eye. "I can't imagine your wife will be happy about you abandoning her bed for mine."

"She'll be happy using my credit cards and living in the style she longs to become accustomed to," Ryuu grumbled. "She can't have everything. Besides, I think she's more in love with the idea of being married than she is with me. We've barely seen each other the last few years."

Kenji worried his bottom lip with his teeth. "I want to stay with you, I do. But I'm not sure I can be your dirty little secret."

"But you'll try? At least give me a chance to make it work?" Ryuu's face lit up. "Please? What do you have to lose? The worst that could happen is we end up apart."

"And go through this again?" They had gravitated closer to each other, almost as if there were a magnetic pull tugging them into proximity whenever one strayed too far. The first icy drops shattered the spell. "We need to get out of the rain."

Ryuu jumped on the opportunity to move to somewhere more private, guiding his lover across the bridge and into a nearby teahouse. "Mmm, this is much better," he murmured, burying his face in the soft hair at the nape of Kenji's neck. "Shall we continue our game?"

The exasperated huff was expected, the wet tongue trailing up his throat was not. "You are so manipulative. You do realize this doesn't change anything?"

"My lover whispers to me." The husky rasp of Ryuu's voice sent a frisson of excitement up Kenji's spine, and he let out a gasp when a wet tongue traced the shell of his ear.

"Soft susurration, feet on *tatami*," he managed, before a hot tongue licked its way into his mouth and obliterated his train of thought.

"Mmmm, you taste so sweet." Ryuu nibbled his way across a prominent collarbone, sucking lightly on the hollow of Kenji's throat and reveling in the throaty moan he got in response. "He pledges his devotion."

"Worshiping me with his touch." Kenji buried bloodless fingers in his lover's unruly hair as their mouths met, swaying up against Ryuu's taller form.

"His passion burns in me."

Kenji pulled away abruptly. "You always do this. Stop seducing me to get your way. You made your choice, you can't have it both ways." The disappointed pout on his lover's face should have swayed him, but recent events left him unsure of its truthfulness. Instead, he felt like the butt of a cruel joke. "He will miss me in the morning?"

"He will miss you in the morning. He will miss you most at night." Ryuu buried his face in the crook of his lover's neck. "I don't want to lose you. Please don't do this."

"You don't have to marry her," Kenji whispered. "Stay with me."

"I can't. They're all depending on me."

"He goes to the one who holds his heart." Kenji's voice cracked, and his eyes were too bright. "I will find a new love."

Hiroshima Prefectural Industrial Promotion Hall

a poem by Jonathan Greenhause

Bats swoop over the dome's light at sunset,
    & curious crabs
cautiously crawl over the smooth concrete below it,
    where a wading pool
reflects the Promethean ripples of a gas-fed flame.

Frogs hop beside the crabs, sharing their crustacean realm,
    as cicadas' ceaseless drone
provides the backdrop to a shroud of spinning bats
    acting out their acrobatics,
their webbed wings resembling gargantuan butterfly shadows,
    their jagged paths
devouring the twilight's boundless abundance of insects.

Long strings of paper cranes are laid beside Sadako's statue,
    & as the day darkens
& spills its countless stars upon the sky,
    a single crane
appears from the distant trees, gracefully circling,
    searching
for someplace to start again,

& it gently alights upon the dome's metal skeleton,
    where possibly
it dreams of its mythologized longevity
    & stares
into the dark-blue August sky.

Tokyo Love Story

flash fiction by Kyle Hemmings

In city windows, our bodies look supersized, our faces, sad steroidal aliens. To whom does each one belong? It's 5:30 a.m. and wet. Sidewalks are wet. I want another cup of coffee, black, no sugar. On a dance floor of spilled liquor and sweat, Zin and I acted out our fantasies of nu-wave love and white swan heartbreak. But now the streets are empty. Echoes are not possible. It would take a person or an animal blinded by loss. Beyond the immediate boroughs, Zin declares that the world is melting, lovers are turning one-dimensional or flat. She's still working on that sci-fi story. We pass an oyster bar, then a small gallery featuring Yohji Yamamoto's photos in a magenta-hued light. I try catching the light rain on my tongue. You don't love me yet, says Zin, because I am too many people. I am every reflection I look at. I am every character I create. No, I say, I've learned to love the cast of characters. Zin covers my ears and says Shhh. Do you hear them? She asks. Behind every door, you can hear the lovers, and in every lover—a secret. Every lover tries to destroy the other because it's a piece of themselves. Then they try to get it all back. A puzzle for two, all jagged spaces intact. Zin walks backwards shooting me a queer gaze that is forced, that tilt of the head that is uniquely Zin when she is philosophical. A car rushes by. She loses her balance, falls from the curb. I rush to grab her. We're both wet, I mean, wetter than what we were in a simple drizzle. With jutted jaw and wide dandelion smile, Zin looks back at me, into my eyes that she always describes as little Neanderthal men who can't make a fire. I smile back, then focus on my hand gripping her upper arm. It must be some kind of love. I can't let go. Not in this story.

Visitors

Riding the Killer Fish
a story by Sylvia Petter

It was a Sunday and I was in the kitchen musing about falling in love with a leprechaun when …

"*Banzai!*"

Globs of green squelched through the air as Ben landed feet first in the shivering jelly of summer fruits. "My chartreuse!" I shrieked only to shake into giggles as I recognized the kimono-clad leprechaun planted arms akimbo in my dessert.

"Oh, Ben. I've missed you so," I blurted. "How's the rainbow business doing? Why are you dressed up like a Samurai?"

Ben climbed out of the bowl of Bohemian glass; he shook as much as he could of the sticky substance from his feet and legs while keeping the hem of his blue and white weave gown hitched high enough to let him get to the edge of the sink without tripping. There he sat, his little legs stretched out to rinse under the running water of the tap I had turned on. "Lots of rainbows these days. But you can't work all the time," he said with a grin. "Sorry about the jelly. Couldn't resist," he twinkled. "All those colors. I was exploring old Japan when I thought I just had to come by and tell you all about it."

I mopped the mucky matter from the kitchen top and took off my soiled red gingham apron. "You could have landed more discreetly," I scolded, suppressing a smile. "Look at all this goo."

Ben ducked his head: "I know. I was trying to keep ahead of the thunder. You know how they do it?"

"Do what?" As I uttered the words, I knew I was caught once again.

"Make the thunder, of course," he said. "They use dried fish hide stretched over the drum, about the size of a timpani drum, but they have three of them. Then they rumble the padded sticks across the hide and let it roll. When they go against the scales, that's when the lightning crackles along with it. When they do it across the scales there's just that low rumble. And there'll probably be a rainbow following it."

I stared at him. I had no idea who "they" were, but somehow, for the first time, I did not want to ask.

"And the only way to drown them out," he said, "is to pierce the hide with a terrible scream."

"But there hasn't been any thunder, Ben," I said, brushing a strand of hair from my face.

"I know. I just wanted to try it out. Just in case …"

He was doing it again. The crazy pictures and adventures, the looping in and out of honeysuckle whims. I hadn't even gone back to the book of verse, the one in which I'd found him snoozing in amongst the musk roses. I hadn't dared go back to open it since the day he'd left to shin back up the rainbow in search of pots of gold. Some things were better left alone. But it was as if he'd heard me missing him.

"It was your chartreuse, I couldn't resist," he said. "Full of rainbow colors, plump apricots, raspberries ripe with juice, crisp green apple slices, smiling strawberries crowned with fresh and tangy leaves of mint. I just wanted to bounce about in it."

"Well, we'd better rinse your kimono and hang it up to dry. You too, by the looks of it." I pointed at the curtain rod and swept the sunny cotton fabric to one side. "Go and sit up there, out of the way while I clean this up," I said and hung the dripping kimono, twice the size of the breadth of my hand, over the kitchen door knob.

Ben took a deep breath and leapt up to the curtain rod, making it in one go and clinging with hands and feet. Proud, he balanced, hanging by the knees, his eyes half closed and his shiny sheaf of barley hair dipping down like silk.

"I'm a sloth," he said, swinging to a stop. He closed his eyes and pretended to be asleep.

I stared at him. He hadn't changed.

"We ate raw fish, you know," he said and flick-flacked onto the kitchen counter.

"Who's we? And when was that?" I said and knew I'd been baited again.

"In old Japan. Down by the village with *Anjin-san*. Chopsticks aren't easy. They're not rounded in Japan and things slip off if you're not careful. Sushi's fine though; you can spear it. Ever tried?"

I had never eaten raw fish. Not that I wouldn't have dared, but where was I to get raw fish in the middle of the countryside? Anyway, I'd never even been to a Japanese restaurant, although there were a couple in Geneva.

"You know, they even have bars where little boats carrying all sorts of fish delicacies and morsels float past before your table to tease your fancy. I could take you to one.." he said leaving questions in the air.

I felt the familiar tug and wondered whether I would ever be able to dismiss this strange little man. "Ben, we've been though this before." Hadn't I sent him on his way to be about his business, to look for his pots of gold. Hadn't he left me last time with a tear in my eye as I watched him climb up a rainbow.

"Why can't I…?" I said.

"You can," Ben said, climbing the set of condiment shelves. Holding the silver pendant dangling from my single hoop earring, he stepped gingerly onto my right shoulder.

"Grow up, I mean."

Ben nuzzled my earlobe and I pretended not to hear the dull and distant rumbling that signalled he would have to be off. "One day you might even ride a killer fish," he whispered, and then he was gone. I raised my eyebrows and shook my head.

Time went by, my career took off and Ben entered my mind only rarely. I had dined several times in the Japanese restaurants in Geneva and had even developed a liking for raw fish. So when my company offered to send me for two weeks to a conference in Japan, I jumped at the chance. It would allow me to eat raw fish in its natural habitat, a Japanese restaurant in the land of the rising sun. It would allow me to test the clichés.

My colleagues had been allotted hotel rooms near the conference site. I was coming in at the last minute, so in a way, I was a free agent. In the short time I would have in Japan I wanted to do things properly. So I booked myself into a *ryokan*. I would take off my shoes, walk barefoot on a *tatami*-covered floor and sleep on a futon. I would wear a *yukata*, sip green tea and eat sushi. I would go native. Suddenly I thought of Ben. He would surely approve.

Don't eat the blowfish, they'd said back in Geneva. Don't touch the Japanese, don't hug them. Thumbs up is not what you think. Armed with all this good advice and thinking of alligators as a mnemonic for how to say thank you, I ventured out on my first night in Kyoto.

Restaurants on the main road near my small side street were lit with bright lights that reflected off the pink plastic prawns and tuna sushi pieces in their windows. I suddenly felt very lonely. Plastic sushi was not what I wanted. Ride a killer fish, Ben had said.

I walked around the block. Close to my *ryokan*, I saw what seemed like a small restaurant. A banner with calligraphy floated down the wall next to a warmly lit window. I peeked inside. Behind a small bar a man was skilleting food on a long hotplate. Two other men were perched at the bar. Behind them were three very low tables. Two were occupied by a man and a woman. One place was left at the bar. I pushed open the door and said hello. The man behind the hotplate nodded. I gestured with my fingers that I wanted food. He nodded again and pointed to the last seat at the bar. Then he pointed at what he was skilleting on the hotplate: a mixture of thin slices of meat and rice, scallions and tomato. I nodded. In no time, he had placed a steaming plate before me and poured a clear liquid into an earthenware cup. I accepted the chopsticks he offered and he smiled.

I ate studiously, concentrating on working the shiny pointed sticks. They were just as Ben had described. The liquid was sake and it made my cheeks hot. I could feel the man watching me. I ate the whole dish and opened my purse. He took 1,000 Yen. *Alligato*, I said. He nodded. I returned the next evening. The man's name was Mitsui-*san* I was told by a patron who spoke some English. Mrs Mitsui appeared. She passed me a dish, watched me eat, nodded slowly.

The next evening, they were waiting for me. Mitsui-san placed a tiny bowl before me. *Fugu*, he said. *Fugu* means blowfish, but the words that flashed across my mind were hara-kiri, sayonara, killer fish. I didn't have the Japanese vocabulary so with my finger I mimed slitting my throat. But I'd paid my bills, written my letters, paid up my insurance, said my goodbyes. Besides, wasn't I immortal? Hadn't Ben told me?

Blowfish is supposed to be served only in specially licensed restaurants because improperly prepared it kills instantaneously, painfully. What was more important? A certificate from experts or my trust in my host? Or the certainty that my time could not have come yet. I suddenly knew I wanted to ride rainbows.

My gaze clung to the look in Mitsui-san's eyes. I feared for a second. Then Mitsui-san put a finger to his lips. Shhh, he said and smiled at me in a way that made me reach out, spear a sliver of fish, bring it to my mouth. It tingled on my tongue with the thrill of taboo. I knew something would happen, and then it did.

A wave rolled beyond the constraints of language. Mitsui-san's eyes told me that I had passed the trust test. He didn't need to be licensed to know how to serve *fugu*. I swallowed and smiled. I made the sign of circling finger and thumb to make it look like a lower-case b. b for "bon". I'd say "bon" in Geneva. But here, the sign would have to do even if my hand was trembling. Mitsui-san's wife patted my hand and poured a beer for herself, for her husband and for me. *Kampai*, they said and we all laughed.

179

I ate with the Mitsuis every day. On the day I left, we hugged. We exchanged gifts. I gave them a story I had written about a leprechaun eating sushi with a Samurai in old Japan. I'd had it translated into Japanese. They gave me a lacquered clay *tanuki*, a plump raccoon dog to bring me luck. Luck had been with me and I had fallen in love -- with Japan -- while riding a killer fish with a leprechaun.

I'm with Baka
flash fiction by Jane Roberts

We're a bottle of Sake down. That's not counting the three bottles each before money-saving bento box noodles in Ueno Park, surrounded by crowds, sitting on *tatami* mats, who are celebrating the arrival of the Sakura blossom. It's called a Hanami festival. Sean says it sounds like salami. Everything's a fast-forward, pause, play, rewind blur: a blitzed burlesque of electric-pulsed Sake framed in pastel pinks. Stumbling over each other's feet, we get frowns from sober-judge pedestrians. An irreverent bouquet of Sake, lovingly entwined with tobacco stench, steams in the air surrounding us, diluting the ephemeral cherry blossom fragrance. That's what we do: we globe-totter around, high up to the gills with local brew, till we can't stand any more - in both senses of the phrase.

We fit right in here, says Sean; he's sometimes fed up with me feeling so very foreign. Sean adapts better than I do. He even knows some Japanese: *Nihonshu. Sake.* He says please and thank you would be a waste of time when the bar staff know you're in need of a prompt beverage. Japanese workers are sensitive to the needs of the tourist, he says.

"There are more pandas at the zoo now", I say. "Can you hear the Bird House? Or we could visit the Kaneiji Temple. It's free admission…"

"Yeah, babe. Yeah, let's do that after another bottle of Shitake", he slurs.

"Or there's the Tokyo Metropolitan Art Museum. Ah… the guidebook says it's closed."

"You want art? I'm gonna pick a word in the dictionary", Sean says, suddenly animated, fishing out our pocket Japanese dictionary from his rucksack.

The print is minute; the word is almost imperceptible to our Sake-goggled retinas.

"I love Japan. Let's make some art", he jabbers on in a throwaway manner at odds with the Japanese bystanders. His expletives catch on the breeze and litter the innocent pink confetti blossom of more than a thousand Sakura trees.

And I love Sean, but he's never told me. He's more intellectual than that.

The tattooist isn't like the guy at home in the UK. He has the air of a master of his trade, bestowing a dignified precision and grace with his artistry. He isn't tattooed; his is a skin—a Fusuma sliding silk screen canvas - emblazoned with elegant characters.

"You're sure you want this, Sir?" He asks for the umpteenth time with unguarded concern.

Sean says that he wants to take a bit of culture home with him; along with the CD of his rendition of "My Way" in that private karaoke booth, a Hello Kitty gum dispenser from a street stall, and however many bottles of Sake the airplane restrictions will allow.

The stench of burning epidermal strata makes me want to hurl, but I keep it all in. Sean has the same queasy look; he doesn't fare as well as me. The events are more inked on the brain than the skin.

Post-kana-branding, a medicinal Sake spree begins. In a strip joint lit up by fluorescent doll-like women in various states of dishabille, Sean removes his shirt mid-dance, the protective cotton wool frees from its surgical tape, and his angry tattoo is exposed. And then everyone's laughing -- the tight suits, the t-shirts and the Harajuku Venus dolls. It's true what they say about Sake: it has the ability to make even the most stiff-shirted business man loose at the collar. That's ironic, adds Sean, because it's made from starch. Sean knows about culture. He's got six and a half Rough Guide travel books. Half of Cuba has suffered from spinal realignment to Lost and Found at Gatwick airport; but the other surviving half has taught Sean a lot about cigars. He didn't need the chapter on rum anyway, he said.

Back in the UK, the alcoholic fantasia of the holiday ebbs away: snapshots of memories are stored in the unreliable filing cabinet of grey matter, the pixels captured on digital memory card, and the Sake bottles gather dust on the window sill, our very own altar to our *ihai*, our short-lived, blotto ancestors. Eventually the dictionary crops up in the harvest of a spring clean. It falls open on a page with a highlighted word.

Baka: ass, jerk, fool, stupid.

Sean still hasn't said he loves me. His tattoo is as fresh on his arm as the blunt stabbing in my chest. Now the sober truth is distilled in my mind, like the gimmick on that t-shirt -- I'm with *baka*.

three haiku
haiku by Neil Schiller

A whispering breath

of rain against my window

tells me sleep is here.

An afternoon sun

stirs the leaves; golden shadows

swirl like Summer snow.

Fallen Winter leaves

are gathered in my garden

like thoughts I won't confront.

Persimmon
a story by Nina Adel

My children are running wild through the huge, new health food supermarket even though the big one has promised to take charge of the little one and not get him all riled up. I am about to try and fill my refrigerator with all the things we need for the week, for school lunches, quick dinners and slow ones, healthy breakfasts, all of that. The only way to make this work is to give them a task, like finding a certain brand of olive oil and comparing it to the same-size container of the store brand of olive oil, then reporting back to me and going back to retrieve the better deal, and I am just about to do this very thing when I see the exotic produce section sprout up in front of me.

The *yuca*, *jicama*, ginger, Asian eggplant, *enoki* mushrooms and several varieties of *chiles* have all made recent appearances on my inadequate kitchen counter. I am about to restock my supply of ginger when my eye catches a particular shade of orange with brown spots, and my heart suddenly lifts, alert. Two-for-five-dollars is really not a justifiable grocery expense for something meaningful only to me, kaki, an obscure fruit here; and anyway, I think no one else would really agree with my off-center use of meaningful alongside nutritious, low-fat, source of omega 3 oils, fiber-rich, autoimmune-boosting and economical.

Nevertheless, I choose two of these fruits and make a quick show of grocery shopping for the sake of the kids, buying only enough for tomorrow, telling them we have to get home, let's go, hurry up, let's be space aliens hurrying to our flying saucer before it takes off without us. The big one rolls her eyes predictably, justifiably, but it works on the little one, who in any case is the one I need to motivate to move faster.

At home, we unload the new, reusable 'green' bags and the kids make off with the overpriced, all-natural mango popsicles I have agreed, in my haste, to buy. But…"Wait, not so fast," I tell them, "I want you to try this fruit!"

My children come and hover around the dining room table while I rinse off the cutting board and a formerly-sharp knife I have saved for

185

years because it, too, is somehow meaningful to me, reminding me of the place I lived and the roommate I had when I first got it. My home is full of things like that, and I have undertaken to inform my children of the stories within each lone earring, chopstick, wooden tobacco box and frayed, ornate slipper they trip over while trying to find something with which to build a fort in the living room.

I slice the orange persimmon, which looks unappetizing to my children, and try to get them to taste this, my history, the years before they came. They refuse, but as they keep their eyes on me, noticing that I am slipping away, I pop one of the slices into my mouth, the other, uncut fruit still in my hand, and in a flash, I am gone.

I am in the Shinjuku neighborhood of Tokyo. From inside this special international phone booth I can't hear what the vendor outside is saying, which I am not advanced enough in my Japanese language studies to understand anyway. Nevertheless, it's obvious that he is selling what seems to me a hot commodity here, beautifully-wrapped packages of tissue, what we call Kleenex in the States. I never use it at home, I just grab for the nearest roll of toilet paper when I need to sneeze. Suddenly I want very much to buy some of those elegant, irresistible little packs…but I can't.

I am on hold. There is an invisible line between Shinjuku in Tokyo and the dormitory at Moscow University which is keeping me and the tissue apart. I'm not concerned that I'll run out of coins while I wait for the operator to connect me. Phone cards and tissue packs are at the top of the list of little gifts that everyone here is always giving to everyone else, and, as a foreigner, I am presumed to be homesick and so given the international phone cards, which only work in these special phone booths.

Shinjuku is outrageous, and the phone booth is a great place from which to view the unusual and entertaining things going on, the 24-hour fashion parade, the stuntmen, the posing teens and circus-like performers. It is too much for the tissue vendor, who moves to another spot and suddenly my sister, studying in the USSR, is on the phone with me.

She says she has looked into it, and it seems that I could get a plane from Tokyo to the far and remote end of Siberia, then catch the Trans-Siberian Railway all the way to Moscow and stay with her in the dorm where she is living. She promises a wonderful time, and I begin to imagine. From the window of the train, Siberia will fly by me in the dead of winter. It's December, and while Tokyo is cold with its homes heated by *kotatsu*—a little hot table covered by a blanket you stick your lower body under - Moscow is going to be pretty tough. She wants to be sure I have warm-enough clothes.

There are obstacles. One of them is money. Here in Tokyo, the money I make teaching two classes every Wednesday pays all my expenses for the week and nothing more. I would have to take on some extra classes, a lot of extras, actually, and then perhaps I could go.

The other obstacle is bigger and more confusing. The real, official reason I am in Japan is to make a record at the invitation of Takashi W., a producer friend of mine. He works for H., a major production company and plays keyboards in the tour band of M., a Japanese pop star. Because of this, and because I am a singer-songwriter from the U.S.—so desirable here—and studied with Takashi some years before at our highly-regarded music college, I was given this opportunity, at no cost to me. I have been freed from the vexing responsibilities of self-promotion. The company has given me a makeup artist for a photo shoot around Tokyo, an arranger, free time in their studio with Takashi at the soundboard. They have invited me to M.'s big stadium concerts and taken pictures of me sitting next to her at her backstage birthday party. They have paid her whole band, guys I've now hung out with in their tour bus, to record my songs. Now I await some sort of decision as to whether they'll sign me to their record label.

It seems like I've been waiting for a really long time, but I'm okay. I have my English classes, my friends to visit who stayed with me in New York and now want to return the favor, feeding me and taking me places. I'm taken to different kinds of restaurants, a place that only serves tempura, ordered individually, piece by piece; and one that serves only things boiled in a miniature cauldron right at the table; another that serves only things either fried or broiled on sticks.

I call H., and in Japanese I am told that yes, they are working on it, working on my record deal, they'll get back to me. Meanwhile I climb more than halfway up Mount Hodaka, the third tallest mountain in the country; I stroll through Ueno Park and spend a few nights at the apartment of the famous friend of an actress who lived in my New York apartment the year before; I am amazed at the 27 TV screens of all sizes mounted on the wall, projecting anything I want to watch from their 1500-title movie library; I sleep in a temple village in a sparse and elegant room, on *tatami* mats, stroll the next day through a misty, ancient graveyard. Again, I call Mr. Y. at the H. company and am told that yes, it may come to be soon, they will call.

Weeks go by, and I am beginning to wonder what I am doing in Japan. I cannot take the trip to Moscow to see my sister because I feel I have to wait for something definite from the H. company. I haven't seen Takashi in a while, and decide to go visit him. I call him, explaining my concern and asking if I can come over, and he gives me the news: there are dozens of words for 'yes' in Japanese, he says, and many of them actually mean 'no'. These, apparently, are the ones I'd been hearing, and not understanding, over the last few weeks. There is no record deal, no reason to stay anymore, nothing to wait for. They liked my music, but after careful study, found it too American for the Japanese public after all. I am ready to go home, I guess, not really up for the speeding train across Siberia anymore. I can't even really remember what I'm doing here, what has occupied my time all these months.

"Come over," says Takashi, still on the line. "We're making some great food, you'll love it. Just hop on the train and come." And so I do.

Outside the train station, I stop and buy a small pack of ingenious Japanese candy, little bears wrapped in edible layers which give way to caramel and then to gum which eventually disappears in your mouth as you chew. I pass the little shops, tiny stationery and meat and noodle and fruit and soap stores which look like they will blow away any second, though they've been standing there for forty years.

The street gives way to fields, and I pass a new pile of enormous radishes I've never seen before, except pureed. What was I expecting? They're like tuna, I think, presumed by the uninformed to be tiny because you only see them in a can, when in fact they are really huge.

After the fields, there are houses in a row, each completely closed off by a courtyard, a garden, a wall. The ugliest of these buildings is made from grey cement. I walk right past it, close enough to touch, and I do. I touch. It is coarse in addition to ugly, and stretches on and on until, finally, there is a break. It is a black iron gate, not wide at all. I stop, I look inside the courtyard at the wall of the house, made of the same grey cement, the garden completely cleared away till spring comes again.

And there it is, a tree, a persimmon tree. I gasp; I feel shock seeing the black, bare bark of the trunk against the grey wall. It's gnarled and jointy. Above are the equally striking winter branches, stripped nearly bare. All that remains is a twist of dry leaves and one enduring, orange, speckled fruit.

I have come all this way to see this tree. It is the most beautiful thing I've ever seen, this tree and what is left of its harvest, this one, brilliant persimmon. *Kaki.*

Three posters from Japan
haiku by Berit Ellingsen

I.

village under white

snow heavy on the gables

footprints closing fast

II.

temple walls at dawn

ripples in the morning lake

cherry blossoms float

III.

green summer bamboo

bowing gently in the breeze

sun dapples the stems

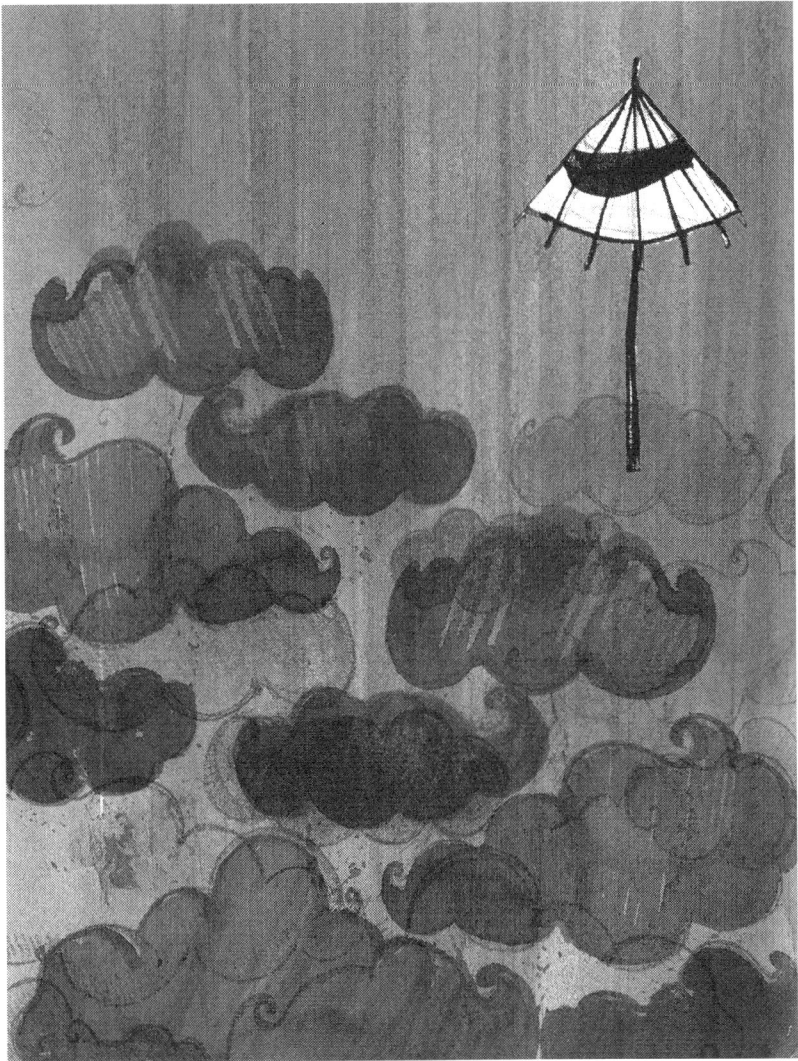

Stormy Weather by Pushpi Bagchi
(gouache, ink)

Bento Boxes
flash fiction by Dave Bonta

Twenty-five years ago I outsourced my motivation to the Japanese. I wore the Kansai humidity like a second skin and shaved my beard to get closer to the soup. I went to all kinds of extremes, even fell in love. Anything to avoid going to class.

Opening a bento was like taking the roof off a cheap apartment building, the kind where you can hear every word through the thin walls but understand nothing. I speak from experience: the woman in the next apartment had a screaming orgasm every afternoon at 3:00. My roommate took to accompanying her on the guitar.

I spent so much time in one noodle bar, an older construction worker became my official sponsor and paid for everything. It didn't matter that we couldn't communicate very well because we had very little to communicate other than respect on my part and kindness on his. The other people in the noodle bar schooled me in how to behave.

Their economy was booming then, and it took a lot of asking around to find where the homeless lived, over near the Osaka zoo, behind a fence: another bento box. I went there with a friend. We sat down on a bench and waited for someone to join us; it didn't take long. He'd come down from the north 16 years before to work at the World's Fair, he said, and never went back.

The only foreigner I met who'd completely mastered the language, modern and classical, was a drunk who went to sleep in the middle of an empty street. Flies, I heard him mutter, why do you always call on me when I'm not home?

Write What You Know
haibun by Mark Kerstetter

I don't know how much more of this I can take. But I'm pretty sure I'll eventually find out. Empathy and sympathy are strong tools and even while admitting the need to sharpen them regularly, we might still ask if we ever know how the other truly feels. But in really beginning to investigate the wormwood, getting past the nauseous sea-smell, and finally making out the green pocks as tiny stars, one can, with practice, send them skipping across the sand. Some become golden disks that burn up over the ocean. Others disappear only to reappear later, most unexpectedly, as decorative motifs for the home. I cannot tell if there is more of the chasing or more of the catching. From my earliest memory I have found only when I have left off the seeking, and yet it is still so hard to let go. I don't know why this is so.

one thousand horses

riant hope riot of foam

stall bucked open

On the train to Otsu Station

flash fiction by James Lloyd Davis

You are on the train to Otsu Station from Tokyo with Teruko. It's your last week in Japan. After five weeks at the Naval Hospital in Yokosuka, your wounds are healed. Three days from this moment, you will be on a plane from Atsugi back to Vietnam. You know that. It should distract you, but you are in love, smiling, watching some children who are sitting across the aisle with their young mother. From their seats by the window, they are watching the land roll by in measures of parcels of farm fields and the rolling chaos of hills covered in trees.

Teruko sits across from you and through the window beside her, watches the morning fall away behind the measure of her eyes. You remember how you were balanced as lovers on the long arc of the night before. This morning, you watch her in silence. You only want to memorize her face, every snapshot blink of her beautiful eyes, every sudden movement of her sweet, warm, wondering eyes. Her silence is a prelude to the remembrance you will have of this moment some thirty years later.

Across the aisle, the mother says, "Mida," pointing to something in the distance. You look back over to see. Her young children follow the direction of her finger. "Mida," she says again and points to something you cannot see. You wonder about the word, 'mida'. You know a word in Spanish, '*mira*', pronounced the same way, 'mee'-da'. It means 'look', and that's why you looked back. It fits the mother's gesture, but this is not Spain.

"What does 'mida' mean?" You quietly ask Teruko, "What …"

Before you can finish, she says, "Amitabha," as if you should already know. Because you are so completely overwhelmed with love for her, you ask no more, but study her lips instead, and the tiny wrinkles at the corner of her mouth, the scars of her persistent smile.

Only years later, when you read the story of the Pure Land in a book, you will finally learn that Mida is another name for the bodhisattva Amitabha. When you do, this moment will come back to you in a flash, a poor man's *satori*. You will remember this day on the train and Teruko's response to your question. You will assume, then, that the train had passed one of those beautiful shrines you can see all over Japan, the ones that suddenly, unexpectedly appear like pearls in oysters, gems in the middle of nothing in nowhere. It will all immediately make sense to you in the future, the word that you heard, 'Mida', and the reality of something you never actually saw and did not really understand.

You will remember, then, how all the world was peaceful in that moment, golden with the glow of morning as the train sped on to Otsu Station. You will remember Teruko's passive calm. You will thereafter imagine how, even back then, long before you ever understood, that you actually looked forward, somehow, to the Pure Land, without knowing the words, without really knowing it existed. You will imagine that you always knew where the Pure Land could be found, that you found it, that you dwell in the Pure Land.

You will be wrong.

Three days after the morning of the train, when the plane ascends from Atsugi airfield, a nervous soldier sitting in the aisle seat beside you has seen and understood the ribbons on your chest. He knows you must know something and wants to ask you about Vietnam. Trying to find some way to start a conversation, he recalls something he read in a book. He mentions it to you in some anecdotal way, makes a long story of it.

"When you leave Japan," he finally says, "if you should happen to see Mount Fuji, if it's not hidden from sight, or covered in mist, they say you will return. If not, you won't."

You think about Teruko, immediately turn, and through the window, you search.

Osaka Underground
flash fiction by Ted Taylor

"Do you know all the words in English?"

I was in the Indian Consulate to pick up my visa. There was a woman there, vacuuming the carpet in the lobby. This was how she started the conversation.

"Um, no. I probably know less than half," I answered.

She wrinkled her nose and walked into the hall. I too went out, heading to the elevators. When I got on, she was already there.

She didn't look Indian *per se*, and I was sure she wasn't Japanese. "Where are you from?" I asked.

"Tibet"

"Ah…"

On the first floor she told me, "I have to the hoist the flag every morning and now I have to… What's the opposite word of hoist?"

"Take down?" I said, with slight uncertainty in my intonation.

"Oh. That's easy. Do you know the word *über*?"

"Yeah, it means, like, super. But it's German"

"What about *tête-à-tête*?"

"That's French. It means face to face."

"And *Gesundheit*?"

"That's German. It means…"

"Bless you," we say in harmony.

She told me, "There was an American guy yesterday who didn't know most of these words."

"I read a lot I guess."

She moved outside toward the Indian flag hanging near the corner of the building. "It was nice talking to you today. I'm Padmo."

"Ted. Good talking to you Padmo." I bring my hands to *namaste*, and move along the sidewalk.

My steps take me to the other end of the Indian subcontinent to a small Sri Lankan restaurant. I'd found it last Friday before the Kodo show. The owner, knowing I teach yoga in Kyoto, was surprised to see me again. He had made me a veggie curry without my asking, and seemed a little amused when I ordered beer. I ate to the songs of Billie Holiday on the speakers. He asked me a little about my visit to his country two years ago. He told me that it wasn't very safe now.

I have to hurry a little to make it back to Kyoto on time for my *taiko* lesson. The subway isn't crowded yet. I have to stand but I have room to read. When I hit Umeda, I pick up the pace, turning it into mindfulness training by attempting to walk in straight lines without yielding or changing my pace. At one point I decide to look past the backs of the people immediately in front of me and focus instead on the middle distance. After a few seconds of this, something feels strange. I assume it's because this isn't the usual way that one negotiates crowds, and that my eyes are rebelling. Then I realize where I am.

A decade ago, my friend Carlo and I came to this place, in the depths of the subway terminal. It is essentially a huge open space, broken up by tall, white, almost Roman pillars. In our universe, there are an infinite number of points and an infinite number of lines intersecting them. What had so amazed Carlo and I was that people seemed to be moving along every possible line of motion. It is a sight so seemingly impossible that it brought out laughter, then as now. A visual *koan*. So despite the chances of my being late, I stop and watch and marvel. It isn't everyday that the universe takes off her clothes.

Outside Japan

The Present Fallen From the Sky
a story by Dan Holloway

There was Kaori, on what looked like an island in the middle of a room, surrounded by shining pieces that were lit to look like ash, like oyster shells, like cherry blossom, like tears, like pieces of shadows, like splinters of lives. Her eyes were closed but I could see from the way she moved her hands and the creased skin on her forehead that she was looking intently, searching, as though the fingers sifting shards around her were telling her about another place entirely; a landscape years ago or thousands of miles away.

Like she was the day four months ago when I saw her in Victoria Gardens. At first all I saw was the sun bouncing off blood-black hair, and then I saw motion, arms moving over the ground through bags of half-eaten sandwiches and coffee holders. I watched for a moment, figuring she was just another derelict looking for lunch, then she lifted her head and straightened and I could see she was dressed smartly in clothes that looked like they'd been newly-pressed that morning and then her head rocked forward and her hands gripped her shins and her body convulsed-like a snake shedding skin, and she was still. By the time I got to her she was sitting up and her eyes were open. I asked her if she was OK and she looked at me and smiled kind of oddly, like you might if you just found a chocolate brazil in a bag of M&M's.

I asked her if she'd lost something and if she wanted me to help her look for it and she laughed and said, "Hasn't everyone lost something?"

I thought it was a weird thing to say. Weird but slightly kooky in a cool sort of way, so I asked if she wanted to go somewhere for a drink.

"I'm hungry," she said.

"Me too. Let's eat," I replied, and we crossed the twenty metres to Wasabi, packed a tray with sushi, picked up bottles of iced tea and found a concrete ledge in Victoria Gardens to sit and eat. I placed the tray and drinks between us and we ate, the easy noise of chopsticks and cars and launches pulling away from piers taking the place of conversation. When we were through, she stood up and said, "Shall we do this again tomorrow?"

We met every day at Wasabi on Villiers Street, and ate in silence in Victoria Gardens and every day when we'd finished I'd say, "So do you want to go somewhere?" and she'd laugh and say, "I want to go to the sunflower seeds," and we'd finish our lunch, cross over the Hungerford Bridge and walk along the South Bank to Tate Modern where we'd sit in the entrance hall by the exhibit of Ai Wei Wei's hundred million sunflower seeds. For an hour she'd look at them with her head on one side like she was asking them things. She'd never speak but if I ever moved to get up she'd shift and squint, as though a cloud had passed across the sun somewhere inside her. And then, after about an hour, she'd blink and turn around and we'd stand up and she'd say, "So I'll see you tomorrow" in a cadence that made it sound like a question, which it wasn't. We never went to any of the other rooms in the gallery and she never asked anything about me. Not that I asked about her either. We just were together, and that seemed like the way it should be. We would leave the vast entrance to the Turbine Hall and she'd turn left, into the heart of South London, and I'd turn right and walk back west along the river.

Some days I wondered what would happen when the exhibition ended. Would that be the end of things? But I didn't really know what the end of things might mean and I didn't really want to think about it, so I didn't. I just carried on meeting her each day; eating, walking in silence and sitting looking at a hundred million ceramic sunflower seeds.

She was the one who brought up the subject of Ryuichi, about two months after we met. It was as though this fully-formed and packaged memory had been there all along, like a shopping list tucked away at the back of your purse that you stumble upon unexpectedly. She was sitting, drinking her iced tea through a straw, and all of a sudden she opened her mouth and with no warning, no change of expression, out it came.

"You know, I grew up in Kobe," she said. I didn't know. I knew nothing about her, but I didn't interrupt. "There was me, and my parents, and my brother, Ryuichi. He was ten years older than me and sometimes, at dinner, or when we were watching TV, I sensed my parents looking at me like they'd come downstairs one morning to find a strange object in their house. Which was peculiar because, of the two of us, Ryuichi was the odd one. I don't know if this makes any sense, but I never felt like I'd come along late. I always thought Ryuichi had come early, interrupting my parents' lives before they'd even begun. Does that make sense?" But it wasn't a question and she carried on without drawing breath. "He was always writing letters. That's all I really remember about him. I'd go into his room sometimes and he wouldn't notice and I'd watch him hunched at his desk, listening to the sound of his pen scratching. It seemed like every other morning a letter would arrive, from England, in a small envelope with even smaller writing. My parents never asked, but sometimes I did and he'd just shrug.

He was seventeen when he died in the Great Hanshin Earthquake. My father was away on business and I couldn't sleep; I never could when he wasn't there. I'd been up all night thrashing around in bed and pacing my room and my mother had taken me out to walk round and round the neighbourhood and tire me out. We'd left Ryuichi behind. It was before five when we left, but his door was ajar and his light was on, and he was writing. I stopped and watched him for a moment and my mother shouted, 'Come on, Kaori,' and the next time I saw home it was just a place where pieces of stone and wood were all but cleared away, and Ryuichi's body had been dug out and buried. All I could think about was that letter; the one he was writing, the one he never sent. My mother tried to stop me but I ran to where our house had been and threw myself on the ground and I could hear her calling, and then I could hear the sound of her running, and then I could feel her pulling at me but I wouldn't get up; I wouldn't stop looking, because I had to find that letter, I had to know what he said, and I had to send it so the girl in England knew."

She stopped, drew on her straw till air gurgled at the bottom of the bottle and put her head to one side and said, "I have to know what he wanted to say. You know?"

I didn't. Of course I didn't. I'd never been in an earthquake. I'd never lost anyone. I'd never had a brother, or a sister, or even a particularly close friend. I thought about it for a moment and realised as I looked into those strange black eyes that spent so much of the time so far away and other times felt like they'd snuck under my skin, nested there and given birth to a hundred crawling things that were trying to break out of my skin, she was probably the closest thing I'd ever had to a friend.

I asked her if that was why she'd come to England; to try and find the girl her brother had been writing to, but she just smiled and said "Let's go and see the sunflower seeds."

So we slipped back into the same routine as though we'd never had the conversation about Ryuichi. She never talked about him again, or about her parents, or about Kobe or missing letters or strange girlfriends or why she came to England, and she acted as though nothing was different. So I figured who was I to push things and, besides, the Ai Wei Wei exhibition had two months left to run, and the sun was getting warm enough for us to walk by the river without our coats and I felt more and more certain she was becoming a friend and who would want to change all that?

So we carried on, as before.

Until the day I asked Kaori, "So do you want to go somewhere?" and she nodded her head and made a kind of mm-hmm noise and took my hand and walked fast over Hungerford Bridge. Whenever I tried to catch up she would seem to find an extra inch in her stride and I thought she was going to pull my shoulder out of its socket but she wouldn't let go my hand, so I had no choice but to keep up as best I could.

When we got to the other side, we didn't turn left along the Thames Path, but carried straight on into South London. Soon we were past the Royal Festival Hall and the streets were narrow and high and Hungerford Bridge was out of sight, and so was the Eye, and the streets got narrower and narrower until we were in an alley too thin for a car or even a delivery moped if it was bringing really wide pizzas, and she stopped.

"Wait here," she said, "and follow me in two minutes." She opened a large wooden garage door and disappeared into what looked like darkness.

I looked at my watch and I looked at the building, and noticed a plain brass plaque screwed to the bricks that told me it was a gallery and I looked back at my watch and followed the second hand round the face once, and a second time, and then I opened the door.

There was Kaori, on what looked like an island in the middle of a room, surrounded by shining pieces that were lit to look ashen; like oyster shells, like cherry blossom, like tears, like pieces of shadows, like splinters of lives. Her eyes were closed but I could see from the way she moved her hands and the creased skin on her forehead she was looking intently, searching, as though the fingers sifting shards around her were telling her about another place entirely; a landscape years ago or thousands of miles away.

There was a thin metal stand in front of me supporting a piece of white foam board, A4 size. It said: "The Present Fallen from the Sky" and underneath, in bold, Kaori Takahashi (2011), and in smaller writing: "Discs from the hard drives of people from all over the world who died suddenly. Messages never sent. With thanks. With tears. With prayers."

Kaori opened her eyes and flashed me an enormous smile; not the shy, diffident, far off kind of smile she had always given me in the past but an open gesture that filled her whole face and seemed to spread down her neck to her shoulders.

"So I'll see you tomorrow," she said, and she closed her eyes again before I could answer and after a few minutes it was clear she wasn't going to open them again. I stayed there watching her for ten minutes or so; the way she read her surroundings with her fingertips, the way her hair fell and reflected the light from the tiny discs and the way they reflected it back, the way it seemed sometimes she was so comfortable she could have been wearing them as skin.

The next day I waited at Wasabi but she didn't show. After half an hour the guy behind the counter gave me a sympathetic look and I shrugged, and picked up my usual box of sashimi, octopus and tuna *nigri* and a bottle of iced tea and ate and drank in Victoria Gardens. When I'd finished I crossed the Hungerford Bridge and kept walking south. My feet remembered every turn on the way. I opened the door, and inside there was the sign: *The Present Fallen from the Sky, Kaori Takahashi* and there were the thousands of tiny discs lying on the floor, but the only movement was the slight sway of reflected light coming from a flickering bulb. There was no sign of Kaori.

I thought about asking the gallery owner where she'd gone but in the end I just stayed there, looking, for about an hour. And then I left.

The next day I did the same, only this time I smiled at the guy behind the counter in Wasabi as soon as I was in the door and took my lunch straight away. I've done the same for the last three weeks now; eating lunch, walking to the gallery, standing watching the light on the discs, and leaving.

Sometimes I wonder what will happen when the exhibition ends. But I don't wonder too hard.

Green Tea

a poem by Elissa Gordon

for Miyuki

We sat in the window

at a little tea house.

We sipped,

talked of travel,

adventure,

friends made along the way.

We schemed to meet in Ireland

at a bed and breakfast of a family

you'd met.

You dreamed of being a liaison to an enclave

of Japanese in Ireland.

I dreamed of walks in the lush green;

the hills, the streets of small villages,

and tried to imagine your sunny disposition

in the land that brought us Joyce.

I wrinkled my nose and said that I knew

this would be the place to try green tea

but I don't like its grassy bitterness.

Tea from Japan you recommended,

delicate scent and flavour.

You would send me some on your return.

We ate our sandwiches and talked of many things.

In January, I received notice of a package.
When I called the post office
the woman was cheerful.
Don't worry, with international packages
you have 30 days to pick up.

I unpacked
a single-serving tea pot,
sweet flowers painted all around
a mesh insert,
and a box of green tea.

I let it steep.
It was the loveliest liquid.
When I pour,
I imagine that I serve a little
of your grace
with each cup.

Gyoza Express
flash fiction by Marcus Speh

I'm removing the bread and what I have now is the dough. It's shaped like a heart without a purpose, an edge without centre, my dream's nightmarish core. Must take a sip of coffee the sapful spunk, then move on. My road is not thorny, that's for Jesus people, my road is smooth; the surface is specious and no good fumes effluence from it. Above the road a sulky sky curves like a crazy racer on the Hockenheim Ring. The air is full of pretzels. They are served by busty baker women, strapping baker studs and baked with soil of Eden. They're promises dangling from the tree of wisdom and I'm trying to reach them. But I can't because nobody's watching me.

I can't because nobody's watching me. Because to show my tricks, to jump through the burning hoop at highest speed, I need an audience larger than my own. I shake my long hair. I call for war. Peace be with you. I am an *onna-bugeisha* now slurping Ramen in the Japanese restaurant on Old Curfew Street, the place where they smile at you with their naturally narrow eyes wide open and the prices aren't bad at all. I'm Eve and I don't know the name for Eve in Japanese. But I know the prices of apples everywhere.

I sit there and the sun shines out of my arse, like in the stories of ancient heroines who can do no wrong because they were born on the good side of the world, singing my song; a Brahmany kite, a herald of the better, the stronger life. I sit there and I do no harm when a man suddenly runs into my knee, which has been smelling street freedom and perhaps peeked out a bit; my bad. He runs into my knee, my knee retracts and the man goes up in flames, right there and then, right next to my *Gyoza*; my to die for, delicious dumplings. I throw him one and he catches it with his teeth. The people applaud. he's not just a bully he's a performer, a street god, he can balance burning bars with his pectorals. What a Siegfried.

The surprise success has made him mild-mannered and now we snog and share the good beer for a good day and he buys me more *Gyoza* and I let my knee trust him. Good man. He whips out his mobile, his cellular lifeline and makes a call, barking. "Whazzup," I ask and he says, "I just quit my job because how can the going ever get better than this?" He is in tears now, and I tear up too, and the Japanese waiters behind the counter are nodding while their black black hair bobs up and down and they keep the *Gyoza* and the sake coming. My man. My love dumpling. He who lives with me at the centre of the world.

Firefly Child

flash fiction by Esther Madden

The day Keiko left, she'd been creating. Rainbow shades of material, pots of paints and 'Loveheart' sweets spread around the floor had met with the front door of their apartment and jammed it. That was how it started. Steve, tired from long meetings with clients, just wanted to vegetate in front of some mindless pap. He hadn't thought Keiko's latest masterpiece would stop him.

"K?" He saw her through the gap.

"Sieve?" She always pronounced his name 'sieve'. When he'd tried to get her to say 'Steve' she'd told him she'd call him what she liked and if she wanted to call him after something so full of holes, like his brain, then she would.

"K, let me in, can't you?" He caught sight of her in the mirror, kneeling down to stick a piece of lace onto her picture and adjusting it exactly right, and rattled the door.

"K!"

"Patience, Sieve." The implication that he was the one at fault was the last straw. He gave the door one almighty push. It burst open and all Keiko's paints were thrown Jackson Pollock style across everything. Her face was one of pure shock.

Then they argued about 'The State of My Home'. She called it 'Welcoming', he called it 'A Mess'. He said she spent money on 'Unnecessary Tat', which she'd called 'Beautiful Things'.

'People with Important Jobs, who want to come Home to Relax, and Can't because of the Junk in Their Way', she'd called 'Selfish, Pig-men, with No Soul, who should Go Live with their Mothers, deserving No Compassion or Art!' Then she'd walked out.

When she didn't return that night, he almost phoned the police. Only a reversed-charges call from a friend's house stopped him. Down the crackling line Keiko told him she wasn't going back to 'A Philistine'. He said 'Good', he wouldn't let her unless she learnt to 'Grow Up' and be 'More Responsible' and it was useless talking to someone with no notion of 'The Real World'. She slammed the phone down.

The next day he found a message on the answer phone that she'd be round to collect her things. Before she got there, his mother had wheedled him into fumigating the flat of Keiko's infestation. They'd never got on. Every remnant of Keiko was packed away.

He walked into the lounge where it had started. All that was left was his leather chair and his lamp. He sat down and turned the light on. The place looked bare, so he switched it off and sat in darkness.

When they'd first met, he remembered, Keiko drew her Kanji symbol for him; lines sticking out like a cartoon torch.

"'Keiko' can mean all sorts of things in Japanese, but my Kanji is special. It means 'Firefly Child'."

Once, he'd bought her candy floss; a wild moment of elation when she'd agreed to move in with him. She'd used it to teach him about modern art. He'd given it to her to eat, but instead she'd treated it as an ornament and put it in a vase because, she told him, it meant more than sugar on a stick. Even so, one night he'd come home hungry and eaten it. She'd been furious.

He thought about how she'd seen his accountancy work as simply adding numbers but when he'd shown her how it worked she'd seen patterns, a kind of artistry to it. She'd been entranced. She'd seen more to it, had illuminated things he'd never noticed. He'd kept the papers with coffee rings from her mugs.

Something dug into him. He pulled it out. It was a 'Loveheart'. 'Call me', it said. He picked up his mobile. "K, I'm sorry. Please come home."

His Japanese Student Speaks to Him After Class
a poem by Jan D. Hodge

Her soft smile and softer voice,

the downcast of her small dark eyes,

remark that far land she had written of

      in last week's theme:

              cherry blossoms,

waking to the smell of miso soup,

the yakitori shops in narrow streets,

the mountains and pagodas

delicate by sunset.

He hears what she is saying now

as something else he didn't know he knew.

More to himself than her, he answers:

      "So are we all,

              all lonesome homeward."

She knows he has not understood,

      repeats:

              "No. I lost some homework."

Prosaic sense comes through this time.

Assuring her that he'll accept it Monday,

he watches her diminish down the stairs.

Alone, he cannot shake the echoes

of that unspoken phrase he heard,

wonders if he is the stranger

in this the only world he knows.

Plumb Bob and Haiku Islands
by Claire Beynon
(oil, liquin, chinagraph pencil on paper)

Watching 'The Seven Samurai'
flash fiction by Andrew Stancek

I reach for her hand. On the screen the villagers run for their lives. They all think they'll die. She will let me hold her hand during a scene like that. My brother said, "It is a poem," when I saw the film with him. He is four years older and pretty smart. Poems I don't know about but I do know what film a girl will like.

The swords are my favourite. The samurai who falls in love with the village girl even though he is not supposed to, that's what a girl will like. Falling in love, every time.

My brother said, "In Japan they all do exactly what they are supposed to. A village is totally defended, makes no difference, bandits attack it. Samurai know they will die, makes no difference, they defend villagers."

Duty. That's what it's about, duty. My mother is always talking about it. "Father has a duty to send money every month," that's what she says. Then most months I hear her calling him on the phone, yelling he is a deadbeat. The bandits are deadbeats too, but they still do the right thing.

My mother also says, "It's your duty to be a gentleman towards girls." What a laugh. My brother moved out when he was just seventeen and moved in with a girl because he had not been a gentleman. Mother cried first and said, "He is throwing his life away," but then said, "You're a real man, not leaving the girl in the lurch."

Dorota is really good-looking. She has a little bump at the end of her nose and her lashes are the longest I've ever seen. Her hand is a little sweaty but I don't mind.

I lean in and whisper to her, "I would be as good with a sword as Kikuchiyo and handle the longest one." Dorota looks at me and snickers. I say, "I would fight them all off for you. If your father said I could not have you, I'd show him my wounds and my sword, and he'd change his mind." Dorota's laugh tinkles in the theatre and the people behind shush us.

Japan is pretty neat but I am glad we are not there. Dorota would be in a high caste for sure and even if I had a long sword I'd never be able to sit with her. I like this part, too, the farmers singing and planting a new crop. After the movie I'll buy her an ice cream cone. Right thing, like I'm supposed to.

I sure got it good. The best movie in the world, the best-looking girl in the whole school, and she is holding my hand. Duty. Yeah, I'll do my duty.

Please Help Me Find the Dollar I Lost
a poem by Tyson Bley

Godzilla of blue Smurf crotch electro waffle lust
    bugs for Kate Bush occult screwdriver forebrain yew-yaw

struggle for alignment of the internal organs on the Mexican platter
my navel out of danger crafted by the most skilled medieval cosplayer,
    the instant my mom said, 'Get your shit together!'

    put the unstoppable Puppet's boxing glove
    helium speaking those words into perspective –
    insects behind the sunny sitting room window hate
    inundate their feet with Fanta pee try in vain to flee
    feel important when their little hairs singe and smell good
    on the cold radiator

    therefore ideas grow out of acupuncture
their epic sojourn in the crawlspace of the janitor's vintage hessian trousers
to eclipse, to educate, to repeat the mistakes of our nervous system
    a view in three dimensions of the ballad from the balcony
    betraying propellers on the caps on the soft susurrating notes

and now a dollar stays gone, its value a cross-stitched haunting
braces for a life of perpetual hectic roaming on the proboscis
    of my father's broken 1964 Cadillac

Out Of The Blue

a story by Billy O'Callaghan

"You know where you are," says the voice in her mind, "but do you know where you have been?" She turns over onto her side, opens her eyes and tries, in the half-dark of a splintering dawn, to read the titles of the books piled up on the bedside bureau. Stacked spine by spine, latticed with the fracture-creases of much age, she can make out some of the words but not all, and for exercise she tries to fill in the blanks from memory.

Crosswords, Sudoku, word puzzles, even jigsaws; all have their little tricks for training the mind, for keeping it in shape. And every little helps.

The books are second-hand, paperback novels dog-eared and well thumbed, brittle with years, the sort of books that, if scholars are to be believed, qualify at a canter for the trashy end of the scale. Romantic fare crammed full of ripped bodices and heaving bosoms, gaudy Wild West shoot-em-ups, and science fiction that on occasions stands as operatic and at other times becomes dark enough to border on the horrifying. Pulps, nothing more, picked up for mere cents from the throwaway baskets of the side-street charity shops. She justifies their purchases with the logic that they will help improve her English, but she really buys them because she enjoys getting lost among the worlds of their pages. And oddly, she likes the westerns best of all.

The voice in her mind has become a constant companion. Initially, in the first days after she had wakened from her coma, what words bothered at all to surface did so haltingly, in whispers that hardly dared disturb the stillness. Time, though, has bred a confidence and nothing is ever whispered any more. Now, even when it has nothing to say, she can feel it in there, a voice but more than a voice, some monstrous emanation that contents in observing every move she makes, and haunts her. And when it does speak, it sounds brusque and masculine, rough-hewn. She wonders if it might perhaps be the voice of her father, whoever he was, or of some man that she had known from back in the great lost part of her life, but only laughter echoes through that train of thought, a laughter thick with mocking, and with guess-again teasing. As if the only purpose of her body any more is to act as a vessel, willing and able.

"Answer the question," it says now, demanding, even though it must know the answer well enough itself.

Her way of refusal is to sit up. She has learned that it is better to ignore the voice than to argue. But sitting upright causes the light wool blanket and the grey cotton bed sheet to slip away from her body, revealing her nakedness clear to the pocket of her lap. Out of instinct, she draws one stick-like forearm up to cover herself, her right hand cupping the barely notable swell of her left breast, but as a gesture it is ridiculous and one that she immediately abandons. Hiccuping a gurgle of embarrassed breath at her foolishness, she lets her front teeth pinch tiny dimples into the pulp of her bottom lip, but with her arms lowered once more to her sides there is a quite overwhelming sense of revelation, of exposure to the elements, perhaps even to the elemental, and her nakedness feels statuesque and absolute. Her breasts are very small, but well in keeping with her narrow body. Her tiny nipples stiffen against the chill air, and even though she is alone the feeling of embarrassment is slow to abate. In better light, her skin shines pale as opal, suggestively translucent and blemished from within, but for now the thinning dark has oiled her body to a sallow masking hue, and in this darkness she thinks and really believes that it would be possible to pass for anyone at all, any stranger in the world.

Her mouth is dry. She reaches for the glass of water on the bureau but limits herself to small sips. The water is tepid and tastes stale but it softens her tongue and the lining of her throat. Her thirst lingers but retreats further down inside and is no longer unbearable, and after five or six little sips she pulls the glass away from her mouth and sets it back down on the bureau. Her sense of thrift with all things, even water, is an inbuilt one, a reflex action that she does not quite understand but prefers not to question.

She sighs and murmurs a name: "Yukiko Wakahisa."

It falls from her throat, even as a whisper clapping like finger-snaps. Something about the shape and feel of these syllables stirs what can only be a memory, stirs but fails to fully awaken. A piece of paper that she keeps folded away safely in the bureau drawer insists that this is her name, and that may be so but she is not sure. She sees the letters in her mind, the western characters spelling out her identity with awkward ballpoint determination, and she knows that the easy option here would be simply to accept. Official documents do not lie. Yet doubt remains.

Name: Yukiko Wakahisa. Ethnicity: Japanese. Date of Birth: circa 1990. Height, Weight, Eye-colour, etcetera, etcetera. And a greyscale image, faded pale from multiple Xeroxing, of a girl/woman who may or may not be some past rendition of her. Not facts exactly, but best-guess estimates.

Outside, the gleam of a rising sun has already cracked open the edges of the darkness. Nothing moves, and there are no sounds at all to be heard apart from the bare clicking of the small bedside alarm clock as it taps away the seconds and the gently nasal hiss of her own shallow breathing. She rearranges the pillows so as to grant better support to the small of her back and makes the best of the short blanket across her legs. Weariness tugs at her senses but she has already slept for almost five hours and that much rest will prove more than enough to see her through the day. Perhaps the coma has, in its own weird way, sated her of the need for sleep, or perhaps her former life has trained her to this state. And actually, the less she sleeps, at least after a certain quota, the better. Too much slumber tends to strip away her defences and gives the voice a free reign over her mind. With slender shoulders bunched against the cold, she sits and studies the rhombic void of sky beyond the window, watching how time tempers the night's blackness down to softer, muddier shades of grey. She knows these shades, has seen them before, often. They are the particular colours of a city dawn, wood ash infused with the bloody and pinkish rose petals of a new day. That seems like a memory too, and acknowledging that and hoping for a kind of understanding, she reaches for more, but the details refuse to focus.

"Do you know where you have been?"

She has the urge to smoke a cigarette but instead settles for another sip of water. It does nothing to ease the craving but it is all that she can think of to do. She holds some of the water in her mouth, tasting the bitter earthy nitrates against the back of her throat, and hears the question repeat itself. But she will not reply. Even if she could, she won't. Because even those questions that can be answered only ever lead in the end to ones that can't or should not be, and because some questions can actually uncover too much. Better, at times, to let things lie, to let what has already been lost remain so. Not knowing where she has been implies that she can never know where she is going, and even more importantly, who she even is.

Yukiko Wakahisa is an answer of sorts, but even that asks more than it tells.

The doctors do not help. Their answers are pat, balms that work on surface damage but which do not heal to any significant depth. Confusion is part of growing up; a time when dreams seem real and memories seem like lies, or fantasies of the worst kind. That is what the doctors say. "Try not to worry; time will fix everything." She wishes that she could take some comfort from this assurance, but since waking, her experience has been the very opposite of such promises. For her, the passage of time feels like an ever-thickening fog. The more she learns, the less she seems to know. The few memories she does hold -- if that indeed is what they even are, memories and not mere fantasy -- tend to come upon her in wisps, frail and tenuous things that flap and bother her but which fall apart at the least touch. Only their vibrations linger, like the haunting echo-notes of a meditation bell. Nothing can be trusted except what she might feel beneath her hand.

Fighting off the sense that she has just dropped out of the sky, she sips the water and tries to imagine a better place than this. A beach perhaps, somewhere deserted where she can run, play, swim in the clear sea, and afterwards relax beneath a warm sun. She knows exactly how the water will feel against her body, its chill drawing a rash of goosebumps across her flesh, filling her with an invigorating sense of being and leaving a salty residue when, later, she decides to stretch out in the sand to bathe. In her limited experience it is far easier to imagine than to remember.

Beyond the window, the world stirs to life. A skin of cloud has glazed the sky, baking the blue nearly colourless. If darkness were coming instead of going, it would be the sort of night that keeps its stars hidden. Far below, the main road carries the muted rumble of engine noise, the first big delivery trucks in a long, staggered convoy traipsing their way out of the city to destinations set beyond the pale. In another hour, everything will again be as it always is, and no detail as insignificant as a mere lost or forgotten soul will matter. Perhaps that is what makes this dawn hour so precious.

*

There are occasions when worlds overlap. This is proven truth; even scientists admit to it. Not worlds as in planets spread light years apart but worlds held separate from one another by the gauzy walls of time. There is the present, and then there are the many, many presents that have combined, by design or otherwise, to make up the past. Very occasionally, though, something happens, some slip in the continuum, and suddenly, often just for an instant, the past rises up and again becomes the here and now. People recognise it, or sense it, but it happens at great speed, is here and then just as quickly gone again, leaving behind nothing but that feeling of disquiet, that churning in the stomach, that overpowering notion of déjà vu.

For those who have lost or misplaced their past, as in the situation of the young woman who may or may not be Yukiko Wakahisa, every step taken into every single day is marked and marred by a déjà vu that has mutated into a wild Benzedrine-fed fury of things that feel as real as breath and yet surely cannot be.

Out in the world, ten or twenty paces along a cold, wet Dublin city street, and already she is spinning, turning for and being turned by each of a thousand small new wonders that snare her attention. So much to see, so many small curiosities. Broken daffodils with their own story to tell, bobbing and tossing about in the dirty chasing runnels of a rain-clogged gutter. The heavyset girl with the long black plaited ponytail and the golden front tooth trying to fly-pitch sodden copies of the latest Big Issue to disinterested passers-by. An infant in a stroller, wetly gnawing on a plastic black and white toy cow. And so many people, so many pinched expressions, so much steeling against pain.

Turned by this world, she is carried along, her cerise pink plastic raincoat billowing out from her narrow body with each new pirouette, her tense hands braced against the air for balance. Her pretty mouth pops little prayerful shapes that hold as hardly more than breath and are quickly smothered by the din of the traffic-heavy street, and there is just the most immense feeling of being lost, of having been dropped from a height into what seems to her a carnage of exotism and abandoned to either await her end or to survive as best she can. Her mind is flushed with terror and exhilaration, and desperate to understand all the secrets of her surround, her eyes, lightened a strain to the colour of molasses in this washed-out glare of day, dilate as they feast on every detail, however seemingly obscure or insignificant.

She is searching. A street this busy must be stacked with answers, and she is sure, or not sure but hopeful, that she will recognise them when they break apart for her. Every window and doorway, every different-coloured different-shaped face a potential secret waiting to hatch. She spins on, pink inside the whiteness of the day, absorbing every broadside detail, holding to the hope, the prayer, the desperate longing that somewhere along this street, or on one of these streets, she will discover something of genuine worth. Amongst so many people, perhaps she will find herself.

People close by watch her approach but look away as she passes, embarrassed or perhaps afraid that she might ask them for help. Huddles of young kids laugh at her. One boy breaks from his group, moves up close behind her and to bleats of gang laughter simulates the act of sex, his arms entwining air, his hips bucking madly. Further along, a teenage girl hustles the attentions of her friends by using the tips of her index fingers to draw the flesh at the corners of her eyes out and upwards. The Japanese girl continues on her way, unaware of the ridicule, spinning down one street and up another, bouncing in and out of shops, buying what little she needs, and her great molasses eyes are always huge, her lips jog and flitter with words that nobody can hear or understand.

The afternoon brings rain and in minutes she is soaked through, despite the fact that she is wearing a raincoat. It is a cheap garment and provides no protection from the elements. But she does not mind. She bought it only because she could afford it, and because she likes the colour. When she has all she needs, she stops her spinning to count out the loose change in her jeans pocket and sees that she can either treat herself to a cup of coffee or else take the bus back to her apartment. She cannot do both. She stands in the street for a minute or so, trying to decide, then opts for the coffee. She will have to walk home.

She sits alone at a table for two and nurses a small Americano for almost half an hour. There are only a few other customers, two separate couples and a rough looking middle-aged man seated at the back of the room who appears to be asleep over a folded newspaper. The sole member of staff on duty today is a young man with a willowy physique, rounded shoulders and a worried brow. He circles, using an old cloth to wipe down tables that seem already clean, and generally just trying to look busy or trying perhaps to kill time until the end of his shift. She catches him glancing at her from the corner of his eye, and the second or third time he does this she smiles. He fights off his uncertainty and smiles back. A few minutes later, one of the couples get up and leave, giving him something of consequence to do. He cleans their table, takes the cups into the kitchen and washes them. Then he pours a fresh Americano, selects a blueberry muffin from the display cabinet and brings them to her table. She looks up.

"I thought you might like a fresh cup," he says. His voice is soft and unsure of itself. She can hear, or perhaps feel, a quiver running through his words.

She reaches for her purse, unclasps it and begins to fumble with her fingertips through the dark silken innards. There is no money there, but she looks anyway. She can 't stop looking.

"I am sorry," she whispers at last, surprised to find that she is close to tears. "I cannot pay for this. Please, take it back."

*

When she finally makes it back to the flat that she is renting, darkness is once more beginning to take hold. She lays out the few meagre purchases she has made on the small fold-out dinner table with the pale blue plastic veneer marked beyond repair by years burdened with hot pans and coffee cups. Toothpaste, a pack of the cigarettes that she has been craving for so long, a pint of full-fat milk, two single-serving tins, one of tuna, the other of salmon, and two more ragged charity shop paperbacks.

The voice speaks, bullying with its usual and interminable line of questioning. This time, too weary not to be annoyed, she clears her throat and answers. "I am who I am," she says, trying with all her heart to believe it. "And I have been to hell and back." She sighs, feeling the flutter of her breath working up through her like a shunt from a pump, and allows some seconds for rebuttal. But the voice, obviously taken aback, has said its piece for tonight. Suppressing a smile, she rises from the table, gathers the two paperbacks and crosses the room to arrange them with the others.

Waiting
haiku by Jennifer Domingo

inbox full of spam

your email arrives

my mouse is moist

Kitsune

a story by Moxie Mezcal

Marcus Moon's eyes fluttered open as he sat upright in a bed that was too low to the ground to be his own. Naked, groggy, disoriented, and severely hung over, he struggled to take stock of his surroundings. Light filtered into the room through the rice paper *shōji* that served as shade for the full-wall windows to his left. To his right were a couple more sliding wood-framed shōji doors. A potted bamboo sat in the far corner, a plasma television was bolted to the wall opposite him, and beside it hung a wall scroll with a black-and-white line painting of a nine-tailed white fox with kanji characters running vertically along its edge. Beside his bed was a wall-mounted phone with an instruction placard that read: Dial 0 for Front Desk.

Shit, is this a hotel room? he thought. Am I in Japan?

Without bothering to clothe or cover himself, he clambered to his feet and crossed the room, ignoring the buzzing in his head and nauseous tempest swelling inside his gut. He slid the shade back from the window and saw Geary Boulevard on his left, running alongside the Miyoko and Kinetsu Malls in front of him, and the Peace Pagoda jutting up from the plaza between them.

San Francisco.

He left the bedroom and hunted around the rest of the suite for his clothes, which he soon found draped over a chaise lounge in the living room. He picked up his jeans and slid them on, then noticed the pair of panties that had been hidden underneath, cotton briefs with little cartoon Badtz-Maru penguins. And suddenly he realized the buzzing noise that had been stuck in the back of his head was actually the sound of water running through pipes in the bathroom.

Instinctively, he started searching for his gun, but it quickly dawned on him just how ridiculous that was. If the person in the bathroom had meant to to kill him, they'd have just done it while he was passed out cold and not bothered freshening up first.

"Uh, hello," he ventured along with a tentative knock on the bathroom door. There was no answer, so he tried the knob and found it unlocked.

The door opened into a spacious black marble room that housed the sink and vanity mirror and led to two adjacent rooms, one for the toilet and the other for the Japanese-style bath and shower. The door to the latter was clear glass, and immediately his eyes fell upon the figure visible through it--a woman, pale and slender, seated with her back to him on a short wooden stool, ladling water onto herself with a small wooden bucket that she filled from the running faucet.

"Oh, sorry," Marcus said abruptly and retreated back out of the bathroom.

"No worries," the woman called back through the hastily-shut outer door, a touch of amusement in her voice. Marcus hesitated a moment, then replied back, "Um, not to be rude or anything, but who are you?"

"Mae Kitsune," the woman responded with a giggle. "With an e, like Mae West."

"Oh," he responded, then as an after-thought, added, "I'm Marcus."

"I know. You already told me at the bar last night. You know, before you got totally hammered."

Deciding that would have to suffice for introductions, at least for the moment, he returned to the sundry clothes strewn about the living room, separated his from hers, and finished dressing himself. Feeling the bulge of his cell phone in his jeans pocket, he had a brainstorm and googled Mae Kitsune, San Francisco. The top hit was a Facebook profile; he clicked it and saw that the most recent update had been a set of photos posted last weekend in an album tagged Homecoming Dance.

Oh shit, he thought to himself as he pocketed his cell and proceeded to search around frantically for some hints as to what might have transpired last night. There were a few bottles of sake in the trash cans along with, he noted pointedly, no condom wrappers. Which was either a good thing or possibly a really, really bad thing.

Mae emerged from the bathroom a few minutes later wrapped in one of the hotel's white cotton towels. She was petite, probably not an inch over five feet, with short hair that'd been bleached completely white--not blond, not platinum, white. Which, along with pink colored contacts, her ghostly complexion, shaved-off eyebrows, and narrow features, made her look eerily like an albino feeder mouse.

"Wow, you look really--" he hesitated, then sighed, "young." Deflating a bit, he asked, "So don't take this the wrong way, but what exactly happened last night?"

She flashed him a knowing grin that couldn't help but come across as forced on someone her age. "Don't worry, you passed out before anything happened. At least, anything serious enough to get you arrested."

"We met at a bar?" he replied, the sentence hovering uncertainly somewhere between question and statement. Reaching back, he started to remember the place, a cramped little *izakaya* dive in Japantown. He was sitting at the bar, checking his watch obsessively and taking the occasional sip of his Sapporo, when he noticed the young woman staring at him from the corner. After that things got hazy, but the throbbing in his head suggested that quite a bit more than a glass of Sapporo was involved. He continued, "I was supposed to meet someone there, but they never showed."

"Well, you met me," she replied.

"Yeah, but I'm in town on business. I was supposed to meet my contact for a potential buyer."

"And you did." She nodded to him, pointedly. "I just didn't see any reason to rush right into business."

Skeptically, he asked, "Are you saying you work for Mr. Ma--"

"Yes," she cut him off, "and my employer likes to vet any new business partner on a personal level before starting negotiations." She paused for a moment, watching him puzzle over the situation, then asked, "Did you bring the artifact with you?"

"Yeah, it's in town," he answered, "but I don't have it on me. It's stored away somewhere safe."

"Probably a smart move, given the sensitivity of the item," she said. "How about we grab a bite to eat while we discuss what happens next? I'm simply ravenous."

She emphasized the last word with a wolfish little grin.

Twenty minutes later they were perched side by side at a sushi bar, Mae devouring a seemingly endless stream of *inarizushi* while Marcus picked half-heartedly at some *nigiri*.

"So when do I get to meet him? Your employer, I mean," he asked barely above a whisper, trying to keep as low a profile as a six-foot-plus former Navy Seal having lunch with a sixteen year old Japanese girl possibly could.

"He was supposed to meet up with us this morning, but he got called away unexpectedly on business. He should be back in town tomorrow, though."

She pinched another of the fried tofu pouches between her white-painted fingernails and popped it into her mouth whole. She was dressed in the same outfit she'd worn at the bar last night, which consisted mostly of a long off-the-shoulder t-shirt with a picture of Pam Grier as Foxy Brown. The shirt was long enough on her petite frame that she wore it as a dress, cinched at the waist with a fat white patent leather belt and a pair of matching go-go boots. Black lipstick and a liberal amount smoky charcoal eyeshadow contrasted sharply against her preternaturally pale skin, and in place of eyebrows she'd affixed a series of small paste gems arranged as two arches over her eyes.

He asked, "You can't just make the transaction on his behalf?"

She shook her head. "No, but until he returns, he's asked that I put myself at your disposal to keep you entertained…in any way I can."

He ignored the clumsy subtext of her statement and studied her for a moment. As they'd eaten, he'd become aware of a few peculiarities in her manner. For one, she almost never looked him directly in the eyes. Also, she seemed to be perpetually squirming and shifting in her seat, tapping her fingers and shaking her legs with pent-up nervous energy. Back in the suite, he'd written them off as by-products of the awkwardness of their situation. Then he thought they might be indicators of a meth addiction or some other drug habit, but her potent appetite seemed to dispel that. Which left the possibility that she was hiding something.

"And he just assumes I can afford to hang around town waiting for him?"

"Come on, don't be ridiculous," she scoffed. "This thing you're selling, it's not like you can just take it into the corner pawn shop or put it up on eBay and expect to be paid its actual worth. You're courting a very specialized market of people who would even know what it is and could verify its authenticity. Lucky for you, my employer has an interest in artifacts of mythical and religious significance, and he's willing to pay very generously when the right piece catches his eye."

He looked her over skeptically but couldn't fault her assessment. One day of waiting was nothing compared with how much money he'd be walking away from if he left town now.

She seemed to sense that he'd resigned himself to the situation and slipped back into a more casual, conversational tone. "So, how did someone like you happen to come by a piece of the *Sessho-seki*, anyways?"

Taken aback by hearing her name it aloud, he cast a cautious glance around the restaurant. But it was crowded and noisy enough, and no one seemed to be paying an inordinate amount of attention to them. "After I left the service, I signed on with this private firm, high level security for cargo being transported by sea. The kind of cargo that never goes through customs or docks at any major port, if you know what I mean. Anyways, on one of the shipments we got attacked. At first we just assumed they were run-of-the-mill pirates, but quickly we realized they were just as well-equipped and well-funded as we were. It was a total wash, both ships ended up going down with hardly any survivors. I made it onto the zodiac raft with one of the suits from the company that'd hired us. He'd only managed to grab a couple of things from the ship, so I figured there must've been a reason those couple things were worth grabbing. By the time the raft reached land, I was the only one on it. Once things settled down I put into a call to a guy I know who'd be able to figure out what the stuff was, how much it was worth, and who'd want to buy it. He set up the deal with your boss, and so now here I am."

"That's quite a story," Mae said. They sat in silence for a moment, then she pushed her stool back from the bar and stood up. "Well I gotta pee. Why don't you take care of the bill, then we'll head back to the room and figure out how we're going to keep you entertained so you don't wander off in boredom."

He watched her cut across the restaurant to the restrooms in the back, then he turned back towards the bar and gestured for the check. Before anyone responded, though, he glanced down and noticed it was already sitting right in front of him on a little plastic tray. He picked it up and saw a message scrawled on the back in pen.

Don't trust her. She's a thief.

Careful not to show any visible reaction, he disinterestedly laid the check back down on the tray and dropped a couple bills on top of it. Then he calmly walked to the exit to wait for Mae, letting his eyes wander around the restaurant haphazardly, playing the part of the put-upon boyfriend waiting for his girl to finish up at the bathroom, giving no indication that he was cataloguing every face in the room.

When he saw her emerge from the restrooms, he made sure to flag her down so she'd head straight for the door without going anywhere near their seats and the check that was still sitting there, untouched.

The first sign that something was wrong at the hotel were the four patrol cars parked out front. Then, when the elevator opened onto their floor, they saw two uniformed officers standing out in the hallway, a few doors down from their suite.

Marcus and Mae strolled by at a normal pace, neither too hurried nor too cautious. As they passed the door, Marcus caught a glimpse in his peripheral vision of what looked suspiciously like a dead naked man standing upright in one of the closets.

"What do you think's going on?" he asked, once back in their room.

"I don't know, but I know a way to find out." She walked over to the phone and called room service. "Hi, this is room eleven-eleven, can you send up a bottle of *nigori sake*?"

"Isn't it a little early to be starting up with that again?" Marcus objected.

She didn't respond, but instead just threw him a wink as she hung up the phone.

Within five minutes the room service waiter had arrived, a scruffy-looking twenty-something with a patchy beard and no less than six different piercings on his face.

"Hair of the dog," Mae explained to the waiter with a flirtatious grin while signing for the bill, her voice raising about two octaves higher than normal. Then, in the same giggly schoolgirl cadence, she added, "Hey, do you know anything about what's going on down the hall?"

"What, you mean with the cops?" the waiter grunted.

"Yeah, it was totally freaky, we stepped off the elevator and all of a sudden, bam, it's like CSI."

"Dude died last night," he explained. "Hanged himself in the closet."

"Suicide?"

"No," the waiter responded, his face lighting up with faux worldliness like a ten year old boy telling his friends about the magazines he found under his older brother's mattress. "He was trying to choke himself while he jacked off, like that dude from *Kill Bill*. He had tied his belt to the closet rod and looped it around his neck."

"No way," Mae responded with a level of starry-eyed astonishment that strained credibility.

The waiter gave a cocky little shrug, as if to suggest he was not impressed, being so personally acquainted with the harsher facts of life as he was. "They say it must've happened last night, but no one heard him. One of the maids found him this morning."

"Crazy," she said, shaking her head as she slammed the door shut in the waiter's face, who hadn't until that moment realized she had even been walking him out of the room as they talked.

Inside, Mae spun around on her heels to face Marcus, beaming triumphantly.

Marcus left Mae upstairs to amuse herself with her bottle of sake and smug self-satisfaction while he went off to kill time in the hotel's fitness center.

The center was empty except for one other person, an older Japanese man ambling along at a leisurely pace on one of the treadmills.

Marcus didn't feel like company, so after stretching, he started off on the leg press machine on the other side of the room.

Just as soon as he had started into his reps, however, the old man moved over and sat at the rowing machine next to Marcus. He didn't start using the machine, though, just sat and watched the younger man. After a couple uncomfortable minutes, the old man finally spoke, "You an Indian?"

Marcus glance sideways at him and continued doing his presses. He toyed for a moment with the idea of not answering, just ignoring him and hoping he'd go away.

The man was short but thickly built with dark, weather-beaten skin and sparse tufts of white hair, wearing a Van Halen t-shirt and a pair of well-worn sweatpants. Marcus pegged him in his sixties, the kind of guy who used to be in shape but hadn't been in quite some time, though he still liked to hang out at the gym and shoot the shit with the young guys.

"Yeah," Marcus finally answered. "Lakota."

"Thought so. Lotsa people can't tell the difference between a Mexican and an Indian, but I can. Just like lotsa people can't tell the difference between Japanese and Chinese."

Marcus gave the man a single nod, not as a sign that he particularly agreed with what had been said, but more in hopes that some gesture of understanding would be sufficient to make the man go away.

It wasn't.

"That's some nice ink you got there," he continued, pointing out the tattoos on Marcus's arms. "Especially the eagle. That's an important animal for your people, a symbol of strength, courage, and honor. A hero. But then, sometimes the eagle is also just the foil for the mischievous Coyote, a rube to be fooled by the trickster's shrewdness and cunning."

"What, are you a teacher, or something?" Marcus asked, getting irritated.

"Something," the old man replied, flashing Marcus a grin that he couldn't help but think of as wolfish. "The trickster myth is common to many different cultures. In West Africa there was Anansi the spider, only by the time he crossed the Atlantic to this continent he had become Brer Rabbit, later called Bugs Bunny, just as your Coyote came to be named Wile E. Because the trickster, you see, wears many masks. In much of Europe the trickster is a fox instead of a coyote, like France's Reynard. This is also the case for us in Japan. The Greeks named their trickster Hermes, later the Roman Mercury, later the Italian Arlecchino, and later still the English Harlequin. It's fascinating that the myths are so similar, there really are only a handful of stories in the world that we just keep retelling over and over. We're like children asking to be read our favorite bedtime book again, even though we know it can only end one way."

Marcus had reached the end of his tether. "Look, man, I'm just trying to have a nice, quiet workout. Blow off some steam, you know? So if you're selling me something or coming onto me or whatever then just cut to the chase already."

The old man chuckled, not the least bit offended by the outburst. "No, I'm not selling you anything. Rather, giving it away free of charge." He paused for effect, then continued, "I'm giving you advice. The girl you had lunch with today, I do not think you should so readily trust that she is exactly what she seems."

Marcus stopped his presses, letting the weights slam down with a resounding clank.

"You're the one who left the note?" he asked, then paused to think. "You weren't in the restaurant."

He said it with certainty, as fact--not a guess, not a belief.

"How can you be sure?" the man asked.

"I didn't see you. If you'd been there, I'd have seen you. If I'd seen you, I would remember," he replied, again with unflinching confidence.

The old man just waved his hand, as if waving away the whole question of his presence at the restaurant, or lack thereof. "It's a strange business with the man who died on your floor, don't you think? Quite a coincidence."

"What do you mean coincidence?"

The man smiled, a condescending, I-know-something-you-don't kind of smile. "You mean you haven't even bothered to find out who he was?"

"What's it to you, anyways," Marcus snapped, the anger in his voice now evident. "Why are you telling me this, who are you?"

The old man replied, "This is not the first time she's done something like this. She took something from me once, just as she plans to steal the *Sessho-seki* from you. However, being an old man alone with little resources, I have found the best course of revenge is frustrating her efforts to do to others what she did to me."

With that the man rose and left the fitness center. Marcus tried to banish what had been said from his mind and just continue on with his workout. However, the conversation gnawed at him, and finally he admitted that ignoring the warning would be foolish. If there was even the possibility that the girl was setting him up to steal the stone, then of course he should look into it.

So he dug his cell phone out of his gym bag and called Nathan Naglee, his friend who set up the sale.

"So how'd it go? Is it done?" Nate answered, not bothering with pleasantries.

"No," Marcus replied and proceeded to explain about Mae and her absent employer. Then he brought up the dead man.

"I was wondering if you could check into that for me, see if there's any reason I should be concerned?"

"Are you concerned?" Nate asked.

"Not yet. But I got a hunch, something doesn't feel right, and I want to check it out."

He hung up and finished his workout. Just when he was ready to head back up to the suite, Nate called back.

"Your corpse is named Seto Nakamura. He was a doctor of history at Stanford, specializing in pre-feudal Japan. He also had a side business authenticating and appraising Japanese antiques. Quite a coincidence that he happened to die a few doors down from you, considering the specific contraband you are trying to unload."

"Son of a bitch," Marcus hissed. "You think Mae offend him?"

"I don't know that we can jump to that conclusion. But you were supposed to meet an unnamed contact to facilitate the sale of one of the most valuable esoteric artifacts in the world. Instead, you wind up on a play date with little miss homecoming queen while a distinguished scholar chokes to death on his own imitation gator belt. So you tell me, is that reason enough to be concerned for you?"

"Where have you been?" Mae called as she heard the door to the suite swing open.

Marcus walked into the living room and found her sprawled out on the chaise lounge, a paperback book spread open in front of her face. He recognized it as one of his, a hard-boiled detective story a la Raymond Chandler, called Invisible Ink. She must've taken it out of his luggage.

"At the gym," he answered.

"So that's what that smell is." She peeked over the top of the book with a twinkle in her eye.

"Har har, very funny. Don't worry, I'm about to hop in the shower."

She lowered the book onto her lap. "Sounds fun. Need a hand?"

He shook his head. "You can cut the naughty school girl bit, by the way. Not that it isn't very convincing, but I don't exactly have a sweet tooth for jailbait."

"But my employer was very clear that I was to remain at your disposal for any and every--"

"And just where is your employer, by the way?" Marcus cut her off. "Have you heard from him at all today? He is still meeting me tomorrow, right?"

He didn't even wait around for her to come up with a response, he just headed straight for the shower.

A couple minutes later, though, he heard the outer bathroom door creak open, then she appeared in front of the clear glass shower door.

"I wanna see a movie."

He continued soaping himself up, trying to act as nonplussed as possible given the circumstances. "I thought I said I didn't want you in here."

"I know, but I'm bored. I wanna see a movie."

"Then go see a movie."

"I wanna see a movie with you."

Great, he thought. I've traded up from the naughty schoolgirl to the spoiled princess. I can only wonder what mask she'll try on next.

"Just let me finish my shower first," he groaned.

Later, the two of them were sitting in a dark theater, watching Leo DiCaprio and Joe Gordon-Levitt chew up some quasi-Japanese scenery while Chris Nolan convinced himself that turning a camera on its side to film his actors walking on walls was somehow a cinematic breakthrough.

Marcus squirmed in his seat, the plot of the movie overwhelming him in his present state of mind. Deception, betrayal, illusions inside illusions, it was all hitting uncomfortably close to home, and he couldn't stop himself from thinking about his current situation, constantly revisiting and reanalyzing, looking at every angle for some hint at what to believe.

He needed a break, needed to get away from the film's relentless fury of explosion and exposition, to have some quiet time to think, so he excused himself to take a leak.

He was pleased to find the men's room empty, or at least that's how it appeared at first. But seconds after he'd unzipped in front of the urinal, he heard someone stirring in one of the stalls--the distinctive spinning of a toilet paper roll, some grunting, a belt buckle jangling and fabric rustling as pants were hoisted up. Then came the flush, and when the stall door opened to reveal the old man from the fitness center, Marcus was not the least bit surprised.

"I see you're still with her," he said while crossing the restroom to reach the sinks.

"Don't worry on my account, old man," Marcus replied, trying to sound as confident as a man could caught mid-leak." Anything I have that's worth stealing is safely locked away."

The old man ran the sink for a few seconds and gave his hands a perfunctory splashing, then casually said, "That's assuming she hasn't already taken it, of course."

"What do you mean?"

"She knew who you were, what you were in town for, who you were supposed to meet, and where you were supposed to meet him. Isn't it even the slightest bit possible that she knew what flight you'd arrive on, that she'd have been able to watch everything you did between getting off that plane and arriving at the bar, that she'd have seen where you hid it?"

Marcus zipped up and slammed his fist down on the urinal lever to flush. "But even if she knew where it was, it doesn't do her any good without the combination."

"Surely a man with your particular set of life experiences is familiar with drugs, like haloperidol, used in interrogations."

"Yeah, but if she'd drugged me, I'm sure I'd have noticed," he said as he started to wash his hands at a sink, but then cut himself off. He remembered this morning, waking up with a killer hangover, unable to remember what happened last night, even though the more he thought about it, he could have sworn he only had the one glass of Sapporo.

"That bitch," he barked, lifting his eyes up from the sink to look for the old man, but he was gone. Instead of going back to the movie, he hopped a cab to SFO. Once at the airport, he headed for the long-term self-serve storage lockers, found the one he'd rented the day before, and punched in his code. Inside sat a small red metal box, just as he'd left it. He picked it up and opened it, revealing a seemingly nondescript fragment of stone.

It's still here, he chided himself. Stupid, so stupid, of course she hadn't taken it. Even if she was a thief, why would she stick around all day after she already had what she wanted?

Then another thought entered his head, making him grit his teeth in anger. It's the old man, he's the thief. He probably had me followed, and I led him right to it.

He knew it wasn't safe to leave the stone in the locker again, and probably wouldn't even be safe to move it to another hiding place. He'd have to take it with him.

Which left him with two choices, as he saw it. On the one hand, he could call it a wash, cut his losses, and just hop on the first plane back home.

But then on the other hand, he'd be walking away from a fortune if Mae was on the level. And what she'd said earlier was true--there weren't that many other potential buyers who'd be willing to pay top dollar for what he had to sell. Even if Mae was a thief, he might still be able to soldier through and connect with his real buyer. He was pretty confident he could handle whatever was about to be thrown at him, and he had no intention of going home empty-handed.

Once back at the hotel, he figured he'd better play it safe and assume that Mae couldn't be trusted. So before heading upstairs, he stopped by the front desk to tell them he was checking out and ask for a bellhop to bring his bags down from the room.

Once he'd settled up that business, he headed over to the elevators and casually loitered around until he saw the bellhop show up pushing a luggage caddy. He was stocky and solidly built--perfect for Marcus's purposes.

He followed the bellhop into the elevator and, after the other man pressed the button for his floor, made some bland quip about it being convenient they were headed the same way.

Once they reached the floor, he exited ahead of the bellhop and headed to the right, knowing the other man would turn left. He went a few paces down the hallway in the wrong direction, then doubled back to tail his quarry at an inconspicuous distance.

He watched the bellhop swipe his key card in the lock. If Mae was looking to betray him, she'd have realized what was up when he never came back from the bathroom and would probably be waiting inside the suite in case he showed back up. He could picture her, lying in wait on the other side of the door, gun drawn, listening for the telltale beep and click of the door unlocking. Luckily, the portly porter would make an excellent human shield.

But he watched the bellhop open the door and wheel the luggage caddy into the room with no gunshots or commotion. So he sped across the hallway with a few quick strides and managed to stop the door before it locked back into place.

Inside, he didn't see any sign of Mae or any other ambush, just the bellhop looking slightly bemused.

"Is this your room?" he asked as he turned to see Marcus enter. "I'm supposed to be picking up your bags, but nothing seems to be packed."

"Hmm, my girlfriend was supposed to have them ready to go," Marcus replied, affecting a mild irritation in his tone. "Let me see if she's here."

He checked the other rooms--the bedroom, the bathroom--but

she wasn't there. The bellhop gave him a good-natured shrug when he walked back into the living room.

"Well, I can come back in five minutes if you think you'll be ready by then," he offered.

Marcus was about to decline, but then an idea caught hold of him. His eyes wandered over to the closet door, which was closed, and his mind drifted back to the dead professor hanging from the clothes rod. He drew his gun and walked over while the terrified bellhop threw himself on the floor. His first instinct was to just fire blindly into the closed door. In a way it might be the safest move, but if she's not in there--or worse, if she was innocent and tied up inside, or someone else was--it would be an unnecessary risk. Instead, he opted for the compromise, and sent his boot-clad foot flying through the door, splintering the wooden slats. But Marcus's foot didn't connect with anything inside, and he pulled open the door to reveal the empty closet.

He felt the adrenaline drain from his system. He wasn't thinking clearly, he realized. He was too amped up, too pissed, chasing shadows in the dark.

He stood there chiding himself, trying to cool off so he could reassess the situation, and that was when he felt something cold and sharp press into the skin of his neck.

His first thought was how he could have been so stupid as to turn his back on the bellhop. His second was how that fat load managed to sneak up without him hearing.

But as he reeled around and felt the warm jets of blood pump out of his slit throat, it wasn't the bellhop he saw standing behind him, but the old man dressed in the bellhop's uniform.

He tried to open his lips to curse his assailant but the only thing that he managed to get out of his mouth was a sputtering mist of blood.

The old man knelt down and dug the red metal box out of his pocket. He flailed his arms desperately at the man's face in a vain attempt to fight back, but the old man easily swatted him away.

Except, he realized, it wasn't the old man wearing the bellhop's uniform.

It was Mae.

She rose to her feet and looked down at him, regarding him with a mixture of pity and amusement as the life rapidly drained out onto the hotel room carpet.

Then she turned to walk away, and he saw that she'd changed once again. Now instead of the uniform, she was back in the same outfit she'd been wearing since last night--the long Pam Grier t-shirt with the white patent leather belt and matching go-go boots.

And something else was different--though he was certain at this point it must've been delirium, his mind playing tricks on him as it shut itself down--but he could've sworn he saw something that looked like a furry white tail poke out from under the bottom of her shirt, just before she walked out the room and let the door swing shut behind her.

This made him think of the painting in the bedroom of the nine-tailed fox and its kanji characters, which he'd have known, if he'd been able to read them, said: Kitsune.

Blossom Tree by Naomi Houser
(black/white photo)

Contributors

Nina Adel is a writer, singer-songwriter, educator and teaching artist, who was educated at the Berklee College of Music (vocal performance, composition), University of New Mexico (Spanish, English, TESOL) and Belmont University (MA in English/Creative Writing). She received training in aesthetic education from the Leonard Bernstein Center and The Wolf Trap Foundation She has worked as a Spanish-English-Portuguese translator, released three studio-length recordings of original music and founded and directed an arts-based non-profit community organization. Amongst her recent published works are fiction, creative nonfiction, poetry, music, translations and academic articles in the *Louisiana Folklife Journal*, *100 Stories For Haiti*, the *Tennessean*, *Belmont Literary Journal*, *Journal of Postcolonial Cultures and Societie*s and *Poets for Living Water*. She has personal ties to Japan, where she lived, recorded and taught in the past. Amongst her areas of interest are identity, neurodiversity and communication, community-based arts development and the environment. She lives, teaches and writes in Nashville, Tennessee, where she lives with her two children.

Alon Adika lived in Japan for a number of years during which he began learning calligraphy under Nakayama Taigan of Kobe. In addition to calligraphy, he is also interested in photography and writing. He currently resides in New York City.

Pushpi Bagchi is a Communication Designer and is particularly interested in integrating design and education. Her undergrad thesis The Garrulous Gastronaut attempted to introduce children to sustainability and was featured in several national publications. This reinforced her desire to explore whimsical methods of introducing children and adults to current issues that affect our lives.

Sessha Batto is a sword-carrying Buddhist writer of angsty homoerotic fiction. She turned to writing full time after a twenty year stint in video production editing, scripting and creating motion graphics. Originally from Belfast, she lives in the States with her husband, son, very old cat and too many swords.

When **Marianne Betterly** isn't hip hop dancing, baking quiches or traveling the world in search of the best cappuccino, she's writing poetry. She has been published in *Hot Flashes*, *Hot Flashes 2: More Sexy Little Stories and Poems*, *The Legendary* (Slam issue), *The Green Silk Journal*, *Turning a Train of Thought Upside Down: An Anthology of Women's Poetry* and *The Haight Ashbury Literary Journal*. She has received poetry awards from the Dancing Poetry Festival and Writers Digest. She lives in Kensington, CA.

Claire Beynon (http://www.clairebeynon.co.nz) is a writer and artist.

Tyson Bley walks dogs for a living. It is also his hobby, about which he likes to write. Writing is also his hobby. It is his hobby to write about his hobby. He is the author of *Normal Service Will Resume Shortly*, an entertaining book about dog walking. Several other books on this topic have also been published by him. He likes to write less formally, and more hobbyistically, about walking dogs at his blog.

Fritz Bogott writes sincere lies about magic and technology. He lives with his wife and daughters on a hill in southeastern Minnesota.

Dave Bonta lives in Plummer's Hollow, Pennsylvania and online at *Via Negativa*. In college, he spent a formative year in the Kansai region of Japan, where he learned how to eat *natto* and lose staring contests with wooden bodhisattvas. His latest book is a collection of "inaction comics" called *Words on the Street*.

D.R.D. Bruton is both a graduate of Aberdeen University and of Edinburgh College of Art. He won the HISSAC short story competition in 2008 with 'Barken, Mad Sometimes' and has had competition success with Fish Publishing and in the Bridport Prize. He has also had short fiction published in a wide range of magazines including *The Eildon Tree*, *Vestal Review*, *Transmission*, *Cadenza*, *Storyglossia*, *Ranfurly Review*, *The Smoking Poet*, *Flash Magazine*, and *Blood Orange Review*.

Historian, philosopher and humorist, Professor **Dr. Art Bupkis**, is a published children's story writer, novelist, playwright, and poet. He, along with his unnatural twin sister, Sephone Zorro, is a literary ward of L. R. Baxter, a professor at the University of Florida.

Jen Campbell is from the north-east of England and now lives in London. She's the author of *Weird Things Customers Say in Bookshops* (Constable, 2012), and her poetry collection *The Hungry Ghost Festival* is published by The Rialto. She blogs at http://jen-campbell.blogspot.com

Ida Černe is a Serbian immigrant, US ex-pat living in Vienna. A professional translator of poetry, fiction, screenplays (from German, Serbian or Russian into English), her published stories/poems span from The European to the New Southerner. A ghost writer, tour guide, chauffeur, and drama addict, she likes to take naps.

Raven Dane is the UK-based author of the *Legacy of the Dark Kind* series, fantasy spoof, *The Unwise Woman of Fuggis Mire*, and steampunk novel, *Cyrus Darian and the Technomicron*. She has many short stories published, including one in a celebration of forty years of the British Fantasy Society.

James Lloyd Davis, a veteran of the war in Vietnam and former electrician, ship builder, ironworker and engineer currently lives in Ohio. He has returned to writing after a long absence, is working on two novels, and experiments with short fiction in various forms. http://www.jameslloyddavis.com.

Jennifer Domingo is new to the pleasures of haiku. She hopes to continue to learn to master this very intricate and delicate form of poetry. She also enjoys people watching, fiction writing, day dreaming and blogging.

Bard T. Fox Dunham resides outside of Philadelphia PA— author and historian. He's published in over seventy international journals and anthologies and was a finalist in the Copper Nickel Annual Short Story Contest for his story, "The Lady Comes in the Night". He's a cancer survivor. His friends call him fox, being his totem animal, and his motto is: Wrecking civilization one story at a time. http://www.facebook.com/tfoxdunham

Prolific writer and artist **Catherine Edmunds** has more than 400 published works to her name. Solo works include the poetry collection, wormwood, earth and honey and the novel *Small Poisons*, (Circaidy Gregory Press). Her latest novel, *Serpentine* (BeWrite Books), explores what happens when art doesn't only reflect life…but is life itself. http://www.freewebs.com/catherineedmunds/

Damien C. Edwards currently lives in Sydney, Australia. He travels under numerous guises with the hope of eventually becoming one with himself. He writes in a wide gamut of creative disciplines with, among others, a notable exception of play-writing, due to his extreme and obvious level of unsophisticated, unrefined and undeveloped skills in his playwright persona. He desires to work through the problem with his hopes set on miraculously discovering some level of vestigial, atavistic like talent for the art of play, because the irregular periods of attempts don't seem to be paying off much. Follow on Twitter: @damiencedwards. http://damiencedwards.com/

Berit Ellingsen is a Norwegian writer whose stories have appeared in many places, including *Bluestem*, *Asian Cha*, *SmokeLong*, *Metazen* and *decomP*. She was a runner-up in Beate Sigriddaughter's Ghost Story Competition and a semi-finalist in the 2011 Rose Metal Press chapbook competition. Berit's novel, *The Empty City*, is about silence.

Martin Elster, author of *There's a Dog in the Heavens!*, is also a composer and serves as percussionist for the Hartford Symphony Orchestra. His poems have appeared in journals including *The Chimaera*, *The Flea*, *Lucid Rhythms*, *Scarlet Literary Magazine*, *Soundzine*, *Thema*, *Victorian Violet Press*, and in the anthology *Taking Turns: Sonnets from Eratosphere*. His poetry has been nominated for a Pushcart Prize and a Rhysling Poetry Award.

Annie Evett is a prolific scribbler of characters, weaver of stories, wields a balanced editing razor and a mean 6 HB pencil. She is a self proclaimed champion for the return of the short story in its own right. Annie infuses her eclectic writing and artwork with years of teaching, traversing the corporate landscape and motherhood. The creative energy behind the collaborative writing project CYOA (http://chooseyouronlineadventures.com), she has a string of short stories published, is a contributing editor in a variety of anthologies and has a number of brush paintings and sketches published. She also did the section heading brush paintings for this anthology. http://annieevett.com.

Michelle Goode is a writer, script reader, editor and proofreader from Bedfordshire in the UK. Despite having gained a degree in French and Fine Art, a love of writing and editing has won her heart. It was during a year-long trip to Australia in 2008 that Michelle first dabbled with writing and found her calling. During the past four years she's had a comedy radio sketch and four comedy web show episodes produced, two short stories published by Ether Books and has been a finalist for the prestigious Sir Peter Ustinov Television Scriptwriting Award. She is a script reader for The London Screenwriter's Festival, Hollywood-based Screenplayreaders, New Writing South and for private clients via her Writesofluid script reading and editing service. http://writesofluid.com/, http://www .michellegoode.com

Elissa Gordon's poetry mines a childhood spent between New York City and New England and a passion for travel and foreign language. She has been anthologized in *River Poets Journal*, *South Mountain Poets*, *Rutherford Red Wheelbarrow Poets*, *The Stillwater Review*, *Short, Fast & Deadly: Best of 2010*, and *Last Words* (2011), appeared in print issues of *Windmills* (Australia) and *New York Underscore*, a new magazine about New York City life, and online in *The Word Place*, *Shot Glass Journal* and *Short, Fast and Deadly*.

Twice-nominated for a Pushcart, **Jonathan Greenhause** is the author of a chapbook, *Sebastian's Relativity* (published by Anobium Books), and has recently appeared in *The Believer*, *Fjords*, *Going Down Swinging*, *Water~Stone Review*, and others. He was a runner-up in the 2012 Georgetown Review Prize and a semi-finalist for the 2011 Paumanok Poetry Award.

Annie Gustin is Brazilian and has lived in the U.S. since childhood. She has received awards for her work and has published over sixty poems in literary journals, newspapers, and anthologies in the U.S., Japan, and Brazil. She taught Portuguese at Yale University, as well as ESL in the New Haven area, for many years, and, at present, is dedicating her time to creative writing and research. Annie misses her Japanese friends, and is thrilled to be a part of this international, artistic project.

Liz Haigh lives in the north west of England with her husband, two children, one horse and two guinea pigs. She works at a university library, which is her dream job, because she loves books. She taught English for two years in Japan after graduating from university. She remembers the time very fondly and is still in contact with good friends there. Liz has had had several short stories and poems published and is currently working on a novel for young adults.

Kyle Hemmings lives and works in New Jersey. He has been published in *decomP*, *TenPagePress*, *Wigleaf*, *Metazen*, and elsewhere. He is the author of the eBooks, *Tokyo Girls in Science Fiction* and *You Never Die in Wholes*. http://upatbergg asse19.blogspot.com/

Jan D. Hodge has hosted several Japanese students during his teaching career. His poems and essays have appeared in many journals and several textbooks and anthologies.

Dan Holloway runs the literary project *eight cuts gallery*, is a performance poet, and is the author of the novels *Songs from the Other Side of the Wall* and *The Man Who Painted Agnieszka's Shoes*. http://danholloway.wordpress.com/

Naomi Houser is a writer, a student, an actress, a singer, a violinist and a mother as well as a photographer for fun. She pursues the beauty in life where she can find it and takes each day as they come. She sends out her deepest sympathies to those who lost loved ones in this horrific tragedy.

Oonah Joslin was born in Ballymena Northern Ireland and lives in Northumberland, England. She is editor of e-zine *Every Day Poets*, three times winner of MicroHorror and twice honoree in Binnacle Ultra Shorts Competition. Her novella, *A Genie in a Jam*, is serialised at *Bewildering Stories* where it won a place in the *Mariner's Review 2010*. You can find out more about Oonah along with updates to her work at *Parallel Oonahverse*. http://oovj.wordpress.com

American **Suzanne Kamata** has lived in Japan since 1988. She is the author of the novel, *Losing Kei* (Leapfrog Press, 2008) and the short story collection, *The Beautiful One Has Come* (Wyatt-Mackenzie Publishing, 2011). http://www.suzannekamata.com/

Mark Kerstetter is restoring an old house in Florida. His stories and poems have appeared or are forthcoming in *Jerry Jazz Musician*, *Unlikely 2.0*, *Evergreen Review* and other journals. Mark is the former poetry editor of *Escape into Life*. http://www.markerstetter.blogspot.com

Kruti Kothari is a techie who prefers to program her life through different strokes and shades. Sketching and illustrating stories is not only a passion but an escape route from boring codes. unboxedwriters.com/

W.F. Lantry, a native of San Diego, holds a PhD in Creative Writing from the University of Houston. He taught for many years in Europe, and still reminisces about the gorgeous view of the Mediterranean from his classroom window. His publication credits encompass print and online journals and anthologies in more than twenty countries on four continents. Recent honors include the National Hackney Literary Award in Poetry, CutBank Patricia Goedicke Prize, Crucible Editors' Poetry Prize, Lindberg Foundation International Poetry for Peace Prize (in Israel), and Atlanta Review International Publication Prize. *The Language of Birds* (Finishing Line Press 2011), is his lyric retelling of Attar's Conference of the Birds. He currently works in Washington, DC, and is a contributing editor of *Umbrella: A Journal of Poetry and Kindred Prose*. http://wflantry.com/

Marylee MacDonald is the winner of the Barry Hannah Prize, the Matt Clark Prize, the ALR Fiction Award, and Rash Award. Her stories have appeared in *The Yalobusha Review*, *American Literary Review*, *The Broad River Review*, *StoryQuarterly*, *Bellevue Literary Review*, and *Ruminate*. "Ambassador" first appeared in *The Briar Cliff Review*.

Esther Madden lives in Sandhurst, England and has had several short stories published nationally and won prizes for her writing. She is currently trying to save the world by promoting the value of supporting Reading FC through the Supporter's Trust: STAR whilst also working as a Data Administrator for a company that aids agriculture around the globe.

Adnan Mahmutović is a Bosnian Swede, who teaches English literature and Creative Writing at Stockholm University. His first novel *Thinner than a Hair* came out in 2010 with Cinnamon Press, and his collection *How to Fare Well and Stay Fair* came out in November 2012 with Salt Publishing. http://www.adnanmahmutovic.com/

Iain Maloney lives in Aichi, Japan. He has a masters in Creative Writing from the University of Glasgow and is a widely published writer of fiction, non-fiction and poetry. His piece in this book is an extract from the novel *Dog Mountain*, which is available to a good home.

Heidi Mannan lives in the mountains of North Idaho with her husband and son. When she's not busy recording the bizarre encounters of her imagination, she enjoys gluten-free cooking and nature walks. http://www.heidimannan.com/

Friederike Mayröcker, born 1924 in Vienna where she lives, was since 1954 a close friend of Ernst Jandl. She has published around 100 books and has received numerous prizes and awards, including the Georg Büchner Prize in 2001. Her prose and poetry has been translated into several languages. The following works appear in English: *Night Train* (1992); *Heiligenanstalt* (1994); *with each clouded peak* (1998); *peck me up, my wing* (2000); *Raving Language: Selected Poems 1946-2006* (2007); *brütt, or The Sighing Gardens* (2008).

Robert J. McCarter lives in the mountains of Arizona with his wife and dog. Although he currently makes his living as a computer programmer, his heart has always been that of an artist. Whether acting, taking pictures, producing fractal art, or writing he finds his greatest joy in creativity. Robert's first novel, *Shuffled Off: A Ghost's Memoir* is available now from http://www.shuffledoff.com/. "The wry humor and raw emotional truth of JJ's journey will have readers rooting for him from death to eternity." -- Kirkus Review. http://www.robertjmccarter.com/

Vesna McMaster grew up "abroad", and took English Literature at Cambridge. She brought out a collection of short stories in 2003, and has had numerous competition successes and publications. She spent 10 years in Sendai, the tsunami epicentre, and is particularly glad to be part of this Anthology. http://www.vesnamcmaster.com

JL Merrow is that rare beast, an English person who refuses to drink tea. She writes across genres, with a preference for contemporary gay romance and the paranormal, and is frequently accused of humour. Find JL Merrow online at http://www.jlmerrow.com/

Moxie Mezcal is the author of the postmodern pulp novel *CONCRETE UNDERGROUND*, available as a free download from her website at http://www.moxiemezcal.com/. Moxie's works are bawdy pulp frivolities masquerading as high art and should under no circumstances be taken seriously. Moxie lives under an assumed name in San Jose, California.

Lily Mulholland is an Australian short story writer who lives and works in Canberra, Australia, although her soul resides just outside of Hobart, Tasmania, the most beautiful place in the universe. Lily hopes to reunite body and spirit within the next three years. Until then, she calls Canberra home. http://www.lilymulholland.com/

Nora Nadjarian is a poet and writer from the island of Cyprus. She is the author of three collections of poetry and two books of short stories, *Ledra Street* and *Girl, Wolf, Bones*. Her work has been published in Israel, the UK, the USA, Australia and elsewhere. She blogs at http://ww.bettyboopinspired.blogspot.com.

Billy O'Callaghan is the author of two collections, *In Exile* and *In Too Deep*, both published by Mercier Press. His fiction has appeared or is forthcoming in *Alfred Hitchcock Mystery Magazine*, the *Bellevue Literary Review*, *Confrontation*, the *Fiddlehead*, *Hayden's Ferry Review*, the *Los Angeles Review*, *Narrative Magazine*, the *Southeast Review* and numerous other magazines and journals around the world.

Uche Ogbuji was born in Calabar, Nigeria. He lived, among other places, in Egypt and England before settling near Boulder, Colorado where he lives with his wife and four children. Uche is a computer engineer (trained in Nigeria and the USA) and entrepreneur whose abiding passion is poetry. His poems, fusing his native Igbo culture, European Classicism, Western American setting, and Hip-Hop style, have appeared or are forthcoming in journals including *ELF: Eclectic Literary Forum*, *Corium Magazine*, *Soundzine*, *Lucid Rhythms*, *The Flea*, *IthacaLit*, *Unsplendid*, *String Poet*, *Mountain Gazette*, *The Raintown Review*, *Verse Wisconsin*, *YB Poetry* and *Scree*. Keep up with him on Twitter (@uogbuji). http://uche.ogbuji.net/

Brigita Orel has had her stories and poems published in *Rose & Thorn Journal*, *Cantaraville*, *Autumn Sky Poetry*, *Islet*, *The Storm at Galesburg* *anthology*, and other print and online magazines. In 2010, she was nominated for a Pushcart Prize. She studied writing at Swinburne, Australia, and she lives and creates in Slovenia. She blogs at http://bsoulflowers.blogspot.com/

Sylvia Petter is an Australian writer based in Vienna. Her stories appear in her collections, *The Past Present* and *Back Burning*, as well as in the charity anthologies, *100 Stories for Haiti*, *50 Stories for Pakistan* and *100 Stories for Queensland*. She has fond memories of her time in Kyoto in October 1994 when a postcard from *Yomimono* slipped under the door of her *ryokan* to say that a story of hers had been accepted. It was her first print publication. http://www.sylviapetter.com/

Liselotte Pope-Hoffmann is a part-time lecturer in the English Department at Vienna University; she did a PhD on Doris Lessing; and has a wide range of teaching experience in Austria, UK, Ireland and Kenya. Fields of interest: modern literature, gender studies, ESL. A translator and ESL-materials writer, she lives in the Vienna Woods with her husband and two daughters.

Sharon Ratheiser took "O" level art in England and has lived in Vienna, Austria, since 1968 where she has had solo and group exhibitions. She has done correspondence courses in drawing and calligraphy and has attended art classes experimenting with a variety of media (aquarelle, acrylics, oil, chalk pastel, ink) and painting a wide range of themes (including natural history, still life, landscapes, portraits, nudes, and some abstract).

Jane Elizabeth Helen Roberts is a freelance writer living in Shropshire (UK) with a really long name. She has a degree in Classics (Cambridge), yet looks nothing like Socrates. Fact and fiction included in various gent's and women's magazines, ezines and anthologies. Likes pseudonyms and green tea.

David Church Rodríguez , AKA Rabbitz, started writing to avoid having to talk. He currently lives near Paris and has a day job making people happy. He writes ocasionally in Spanish and on twitter as @Rabbitz. His website is http://thewritersays.com

Neil Schiller is an IT consultant and recent PhD graduate, having just finished a thesis on American author Richard Brautigan. "I have primarily been writing short fiction for about ten years and published an ebook collection called *Oblivious* in 2010. It has sold literally tens of copies and was recently shortlisted for obscurity. I also published a collection called *The Haiku Diary* which pretty much documents a year of my life."

Having retired from the University of Kansas in 2001, **Elizabeth Schultz** now balances scholarship on Herman Melville and on the environment with writing essays and poems about the people and places she loves. She has published two critical works on Melville, two collections of poetry, one book of short stories, and published her scholarship and poetry widely. She has also co-organized an international conference on ecocriticism in Beijing and regularly participates in international ecocriticism conferences.

Lisa Scullard, from the UK, wrote her first novel, *Living Hell*, at the age of 18. She studied martial arts for 22 years, including competing in regional and British competitions. Having worked in various jobs including as a ceramic artist, nanny, bartender, motorcycle mechanic, nursing assistant and nightclub bouncer, Lisa now writes and edits full-time. Follow Lisa on Twitter @aka_VoodooSpice and visit her blog at http://voodoo-spice.blogspot.com and her website at http://www.lisascullard.wordpress.com

Shkna 9 began painting in the summer of 2003, with a strong background in drawing. She has a fondness for animals, astrology, consciousness, and espresso. She currently lives north of Detroit with her fiancé and three cats.

Vaishali Shroff has been accused of having a long standing affair with her pen. From having poetry published in newspapers as a teenager to writing movie scripts for animation studios, over a dozen stories for *Chicken Soup* anthologies by Westland Ltd., articles in various parenting magazines, children's stories filmed on www.smories.com, stories and poetry for the English Literature curriculum of the CBSE Education Board, India's Central Board for Secondary Education, she is waiting with twiddling thumbs for the release of her first illustrated book for children with Pratham Books. She also runs a reading and story-telling club for children and uses her toddler as an inspiration to see the world from a whole new perspective. http://eikthirani.wordpress.com

silent lotus is a spiritual advisor, whose poetry has been published in Europe, England, America and Canada. He has resided for a significant portion of his life in the Caribbean and The Netherlands, and for the past twelve years has been living as well in Providence, RI, with the artist Nermin Kura. http://www.silentlotus.net/

Marcus Speh is a German writer who lives in Berlin. His short fiction has been published in *elimae*, *Mad Hatter's Review*, *kill author*, *PANK* and elsewhere. He's been nominated for a Micro Award, two Pushcart Prizes, two Best of the Net awards and two Million Writers Awards, and was longlisted for the Paris Literary Prize. His collection *Thank You For Your Sperm* was published by Mad-Hat Press in 2012. He's never been to Japan, but would like to go there one day. http://www.marcusspeh.com/

Andrew Stancek's recent writing has appeared in *The Linnet's Wings*, *Istanbul Literary Review*, *Wilderness House Literary Review*, *Prime Number Magazine*, *River Poets Journal*, *Camroc Press Review*, *Orion Headless*, *Connotation Press*, *Long Story Short* and *Thunderclap Magazine*, among others. *THIS Literary Magazine* has nominated him for a Pushcart Prize.

Diane Stephenson lives in South Western Ontario, Canada. She has been a born again Christian for over 40 years. She worked in graphic arts for 15 years, has done many types of art throughout her life, but now pours her creativity into writing. http://diane-stephenson.com/

Ted Taylor, a graduate of University of Arizona's esteemed Creative Writing Program, has work appearing frequently in *Kyoto Journal*, *Kansai Time Out*, *The Icebox Haiku Journal* and *Deep Kyoto*, as well as in various print and online publications. A Contributing Editor at *Kyoto Journal*, he won the top prize in the Kyoto International Cultural Association Essay Contest. Currently residing in Japan, he is currently at work on a book about his walking the Shikoku 88 Temple Pilgrimage. http://notesfromthe nog.blogspot.jp.

Donald Jacob Uitvlugt lives somewhere in the middle of the United States, but mostly in a haunted memory palace. He writes what he calls "haiku fiction" -- small stories with big impact. His work has most recently appeared in *Cover of Darkness* and the *Journal of Unlikely*

Entomology, as well as the anthologies *Sparks* and *100 Horrors*. http://www.haikufiction.blogspot.com

Daniel Werneck is an artist and professor in Brazil. He takes care of his wife and two kids, teaches animation at university, makes comics and is currently writing a book about French comics artist Moebius. "When does he sleep?" you might ask. That is actually a pretty good question, to which no one knows the answer.

Simon Paul Wilson was born in England but decided to travel around Asia and forgot to go back. Currently living in Guangzhou, China, his writing has been deeply influenced by Asian culture and authors such as Banana Yoshimoto, Haruki Murakami, Xiaolu Guo and Yoko Ogawa. His first book, *Yuko Zen Is Somewhere Else*, can be found on the Authonomy website and has received high praise and gold medal status. He is now working on a number of projects which go by the names of *See You When the World Ends*, *We Are Blood* and *GhostCityGirl*. When not writing, Simon usually spends his time listening to very loud music while playing air-guitar and other instruments.

Acknowledgements

We would like to acknowledge all the volunteers behind New Sun Rising: Stories for Japan

Frankie Sachs had the idea and started the project, leading it to the end of the first round of editing. Through Dan Holloway's networking, Frankie got a quick lesson in the world of charity anthology organizing from Greg McQueen (creator of 100 Stories for Haiti and 50 Stories for Pakistan). Andrew Brenton stepped up to offer the publishing resources of Endaxi Press. (This, however, was tied to the original deadline which unfortunately we were unable to honour.) Promotional videos were contributed by Greg McQueen, Sessha Batto, Lisa Scullard, That Girl Tyson. Poetry was contributed to the blog by Susan May James, Scott Metz, Lynne Rees and Frankie Sachs. Photography was contributed by Ronnie Niedermeyer. Many of the contributors to the Anthology also contributed further work to the New Sun Rising blog.

The book cover art and design were contributed by Daniel Werneck. The "New Sun Rising" logo used on the blog was created by Bradley Wind. R.B. Wood created the *The Word Count Podcast for Japan* and Daniel Christian created the "New Sun Rising" song. Further members of the team were Jennifer Bogart, Lou Freshwater, Elle Lawliette, Diana Mair, Solange Noir, Toni Rakestraw, and Jane Roberts.

The project was completed by Annie Evett, Michelle Goode, Sylvia Petter, and Vaishali Shroff.

The story of the project and further work by contributors can be seen at http://storiesforjapan.blogspot.com. Thank you, dear Reader, for being part of it all!

Printed in Great Britain
by Amazon.co.uk, Ltd.,
Marston Gate.